Book 1

SOUND INNOVATIONS

for GUITAR

A Revolutionary Method for Individual or Class Instruction

Aaron **STANG** | Bill **PURSE**

Congratulations on your decision to be a musician!

Guitar is one of the most popular and versatile of all instruments. With a guitar you can strum chords and sing, write your own music, play alone, or perform with friends or family. You can join a band or even become a virtuoso guitar star. Would you like to perform, compose, produce records, or go into another area of the music business? Learning guitar can provide a foundation for any career in the music industry. Playing guitar involves artistic inspiration and mastering the right tools and skills. This book is all about providing you with those tools and skills. With your teacher's guidance you will learn critical skills and techniques such as strumming and fingerpicking chords, playing rock and blues riffs, creating your own guitar parts, improvising, reading music and applying practical music theory concepts. The artistic inspiration will come from you.

The accompanying DVD features both authors discussing and demonstrating all notes, chords, concepts and techniques taught in the book. Many of the songs and ensemble pieces are performed live so students can listen to the music; play along, and see important up-close examples of left and right hand technique. Plus, DVD Chapter icons throughout the book clearly indicate the location of all demonstrated examples, songs, and techniques so students can immediately access the relevant DVD information.

The DVD includes recorded accompaniments for every line of music in your *Sound Innovations* book. These recordings can be played with the included SI Player, easily uploaded to your MP3 player or transferred to your computer. Additionally, many CD and DVD players are equipped to play MP3s directly from the disc. To play an accompaniment, simply choose the file that corresponds to the line of music in the book. Each line has been numbered and named for easy reference.

Also included on the DVD is the SI Player *with* Tempo Change Technology. The SI Player features the ability to change the speed of the recordings without changing pitch-slow the tempo down for practice or speed it up to performance tempo! Use this program to easily play the included MP3 files or any audio file on your computer.

Cover guitar photos:
Fender Custom Shop Thinline Telecaster courtesy Fender Musical Instruments
Robert Ruck Classic Guitar courtesy Aaron Stang
Duesenberg Starplayer GTV courtesy of Duesenberg USA
Taylor 614 courtesy of Taylor Guitars
Martin D28 courtesy of Martin Guitars
PRS Santana Model courtesy PRS Guitars

ISBN-10: 0-7390-7790-2
ISBN-13: 978-0-7390-7790-0

CONTENT SUMMARY

This book focuses on real-world guitar skills such as chords, strumming, fingerpicking, rock and blues riffs, creating guitar parts, improvising, reading music, and practical music theory. This content summary provides an easy-to-reference overview of the general learning sequence of skills and concepts.

LEVEL 1

Notes: E, F, G (6th string); A, B, C (5th string)

Rhythms: ♩, ♩, ♪, o, ♩., $\frac{4}{4}$, $\frac{3}{4}$

Chords: E, Am, and Em; "specialty chords" F Flamenco, G Flamenco, Dm/A and Bm/A

Technique & Skills: downstroke (⊓), strumming, fingerpicking, brush stroke (⌇)

Terms & Symbols: accidentals, ♯, ♭, ♮, ⌢, 1st position, 2nd position, repeat signs, 1st and 2nd endings, block chord, arpeggio

Rhythm Guitar Patterns: basic $\frac{4}{4}$ fingerpicking pattern

Music Styles: Flamenco, blues, acoustic fingerstyle

Repertoire: Acoustic Fantasy

LEVEL 2

Notes: D, E, F (4th string); G, A (3rd string)

Chords: E7, G, C, D, A5, A6, D5, D6, E5, E6

Terms & Symbols: chromatic, half step, tonic, key signature, tie, ▬, 𝄽, blues song form, power chord, tie

Technique & Skills: palm mute

Rhythm Guitar Patterns: boogie pattern in A; fingerpicking patterns in $\frac{3}{4}$

Music Styles: Flamenco, bass-line blues riffs, blues boogie, acoustic fingerstyle, folk

Repertoire: The Blues Boogie Rhythm
Plaisir d'Amour

LEVEL 3

Notes: B, C, D (2nd string); E, F, G (1st string)

Rhythms: ♩.

Terms & Symbols: accent, ritardando, blues licks, improvise, lick

Technique & Skills: alternate picking, hammer-on, pull-off, slide, improvisation

Rhythm Guitar Patterns: One-grip blues, blues boogie in A; fingerpicking patterns in $\frac{3}{4}$

Music Styles: traditional, flamenco, classical, acoustic fingerstyle, blues-rock

Repertoire: Amazing Grace
Flamenco Mood
Ode to Joy
One Grip Blues

LEVEL 4

Chords: G7

Rhythms: swing eighth notes

Terms & Symbols: major, minor, dominant 7, (⊘), *D.S. al Coda*, *To Coda*, a tempo, swing feel, staccato, blue notes

Technique & Skills: playing by ear

Music Styles: folk and American traditional, classical, jazz

Repertoire: Simple Gifts
Für Elise
When the Saints Go Marchin' In

LEVEL 5

Chords: G7 (new form), D/F♯, A7, D7, F

Rhythms: ♪

Terms & Symbols: roots music, shuffle, barre

Technique & Skills: shuffle rhythm

Rhythm Guitar Patterns: three-chord rock and roll, alternating thumb, blues shuffle

Music Styles: rock and roll, roots music, blues shuffle

Repertoire: Corinna, Corinna
A Blues Shuffle

LEVEL 6

Rhythms: ♪♪♪

Terms & Symbols: dynamics, *f*, *mf*, *p*, *mp*, triplets

Chords: Dm, B7

Music Styles: classical, blues-rock, Spanish-classical, American traditional

Repertoire: Minuet in G
Aguado Study
One Finger Blues
Romanza
Simple Gifts

APPENDIX 1: Parts of the Guitar

APPENDIX 2: Guitar Types

APPENDIX 3: Holding the Guitar

APPENDIX 4: Technique and Warm-Up Exercises

APPENDIX 5: Tuning the Guitar

APPENDIX 6: Reading Music and Tablature Notation

APPENDIX 7: Reading Rhythm Notation

Level 1: Notes on the 6th and 5th Strings

See appendix 6 for a complete overview of music notation and tablature.

1

FIRST NOTES: E, F, and **G**—These notes are on the 6th string.

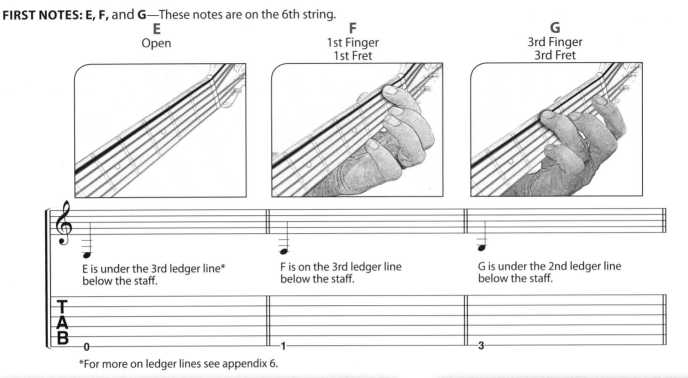

*For more on ledger lines see appendix 6.

QUARTER NOTE ♩ = 1 count (1 +)
HALF NOTE ♪ = 2 counts (1 + 2 +)

4/4 TIME SIGNATURE
4 = Four counts per measure
4 = A quarter note receives one count

TECHNIQUE

- Right hand: Play all notes with a **DOWNSTROKE** of the pick ⊓. Strike the string with a downward attack, towards the floor, coming to rest on the 5th string. The term **SIMILE** means to continue playing in the same manner.

- Left hand: To produce the best tone with the least amount of pressure, place your fingertip directly behind the fret, but not on top of it.

---

2 **FIRST NOTES**—Listen as your teacher counts and plays E, F, and G notes, then echo back each measure. (Count "1 and 2 and 3 and 4 and.")

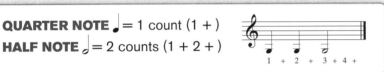

3 **STAY DOWN**—Play F with your 1st finger, and hold it down as you play G. Don't release the F until it's absolutely necessary to play the open E.

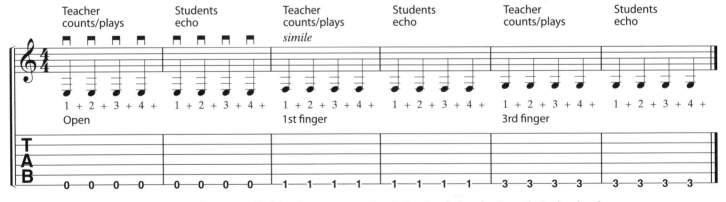

4 **FLAMENCO MOOD**—*Flamenco* is a type of Spanish folk music. Guitar is central to the Flamenco style, which has influenced many other styles of guitar from classical to rock.

A **CHORD** is three or more notes played at the same time. Guitarists often play combinations of chords and single notes.

FIRST CHORD: E—To play the E chord, place your fingers as shown in the diagram, and *strum* through all six strings following the instructions below. (See appendix 6 for how to read chord diagrams.)

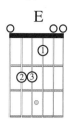

Notice that the lowest note of the E chord (the open 6th string) is E, which is also the name of the chord. The note or letter name of any chord is called the **ROOT**.

To **STRUM** the E chord, position your pick on the low E string, holding it with a very relaxed grip, and allow your hand to *fall* through all six strings, stopping after it passes through the first string (closest to the floor). Then return to astrum again. Don't *push* your hand through; just allow it to drop through the strings to create a single, even sound, not six separate notes.

RHYTHM SLASHES (ʹ) indicate rhythm without showing pitch. They are often used in conjunction with chord diagrams to indicate the rhythmic strum pattern for the chords.

FIRST STRUM—This exercise introduces the E chord.

MOVING CHORDS—Slide the E shape up one fret and play all six strings to create a very interesting chord we will call F Flamenco. Make sure your fingers maintain the E shape as you slide up the strings. Playing all six open strings gives us a chord we will call G Flamenco. These two Flamenco-style chords are not "standard" guitar chord forms, but they sound great and are used in Flamenco guitar.

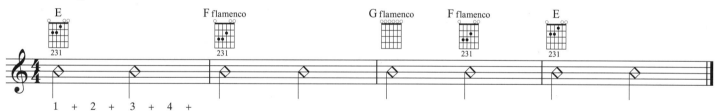

FLAMENCO MOOD (duet)—In this song Guitar 1 plays the melody and Guitar 2 plays the chords. Play along with the CD track. (On the CD, you will first hear the duet, followed by Guitar 2 alone then, Guitar 1 alone.)

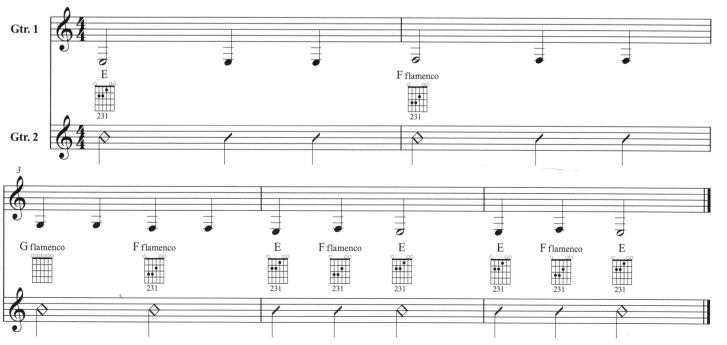

9 NEW NOTES: **A, B,** and **C**—These notes are on the 5th string.

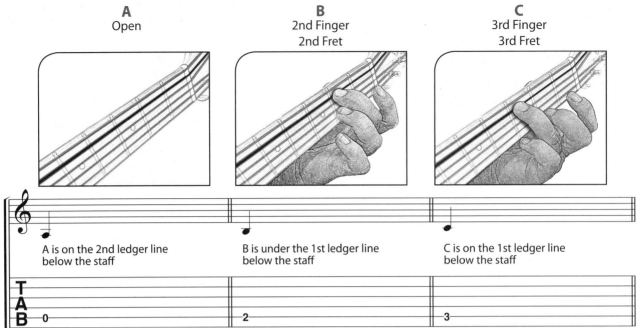

A Open	B 2nd Finger 2nd Fret	C 3rd Finger 3rd Fret

A is on the 2nd ledger line below the staff

B is under the 1st ledger line below the staff

C is on the 1st ledger line below the staff

10 NEW NOTES—Listen as your teacher counts and plays the notes A, B, and C, then echo back each measure.

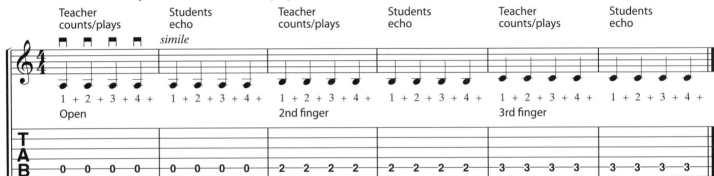

Teacher counts/plays · Students echo · Teacher counts/plays · Students echo · Teacher counts/plays · Students echo

Open · 2nd finger · 3rd finger

11 STILL STAY DOWN—As you ascend from low E to G, keep your 1st finger down on F, and don't lift it until you change strings. As you ascend from low A to C, keep your 2nd finger down on B until you must release it.

An **EIGHTH NOTE** (♪) receives one-half beat. Two eighth notes equal one beat. Eighth notes often appear in pairs or groups of four with a *beam* across the top of the stems (♫). Play the first eighth note on the count and the second eighth note on the "and," represented by a "+" sign in the music.

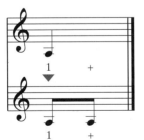
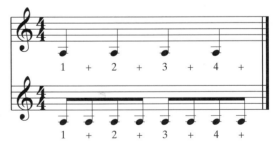

12 EIGHTH NOTE ETUDE—An *etude* is a short exercise composed for a solo instrument that is used to develop a specific technical skill. Play slowly and very evenly. Tap your foot on the count (1–2–3–4) and use all downstrokes.

NEW CHORD: A MINOR—The A minor chord (written as Am) is a five-string chord. Place your fingers as shown in the diagram and strum through five strings, carefully missing the low 6th string. Notice that the Am chord shape and fingering is exactly the same as for the E chord, but on the next set of strings. Also notice that the note A, the name of the chord, is the lowest note in the chord (the open 5th string). Remember: The note name of the chord is called the *root*.

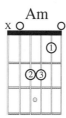

A MINOR ENSEMBLE—Learn and perform both parts of this ensemble. Notice all three chords use the same fingering shape. Maintain this shape when changing from chord to chord.
- **Guitar 1:** The melody part uses all the notes and rhythms you've learned so far.
- **Guitar 2:** When strumming chords, hold your pick with a very relaxed grip and allow your pick hand to fall through the strings—don't push.

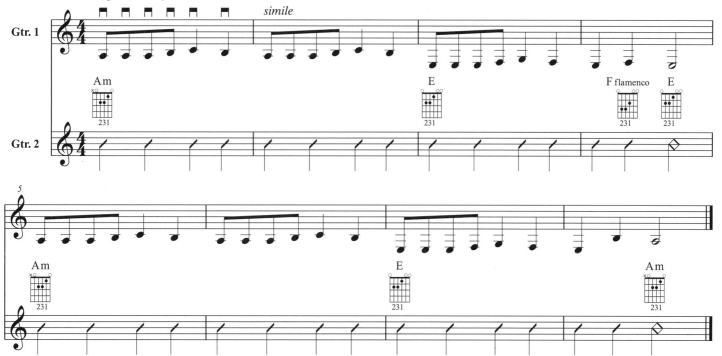

A **FERMATA** (𝄐) means to hold or pause on the note.

DRIVING RHYTHM—Learn and perform both parts of this ensemble.
- **Guitar 1:** The melody is a great technique workout for your left hand.
- **Guitar 2:** The rhythm part uses eighth-note rhythms for the strum. Use all downstrokes, focusing on the lowest three or four strings of each chord to create a low, bass-driven sound.

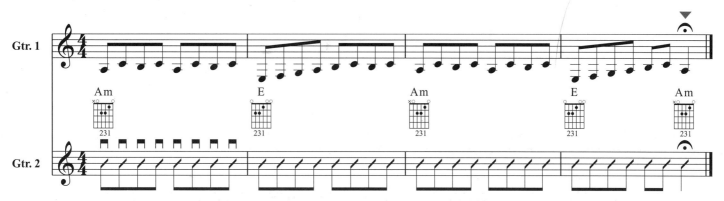

A **SHARP SIGN** (♯) raises a note one half step—exactly one fret up from the *natural* (un-altered) note. A **FLAT SIGN** (♭) lowers a note one half step—exactly one fret down from the natural note. Notice that F♯ and G♭ are just different names for the same exact note. Once indicated, a sharp or flat remains in effect for the rest of the measure and is canceled at the bar line or with a **NATURAL SIGN** (♮). Sharps, flats, and naturals are called **ACCIDENTALS**.

A **RIGHT-FACING REPEAT** indicates the first measure of a section to be repeated.

A **LEFT-FACING REPEAT** indicates to go back to the closest right-facing repeat, or back to the beginning if there is no right-facing repeat.

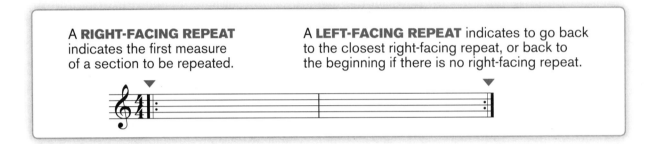

When your hand is positioned on the neck so that your 1st finger is at the 1st fret and your 2nd finger is at the 2nd fret and so on, your hand is in the **1ST POSITION**.

16 **STRENGTH BUILDER**—This exercise is ideal for building strength and dexterity in your left-hand fingers. As you ascend on the 6th string from E to G♯, and on the 5th string from A to C♯, keep each finger down just behind the fret. Do not add or lift any finger until necessary as you ascend and descend the pattern.

A **WHOLE NOTE** (𝗼) receives 4 counts. A whole note in rhythm slash notation looks like this: ◇

A **BRUSH STROKE** (↕) means to rapidly glide your pick down the strings, allowing them to ring.

17 **CRIME THEME NO. 1**—Soundtracks from many of the classic spy and crime dramas of the 1960s feature bluesy guitar bass lines like this one. Guitar 1 plays the bass-line melody. Guitar 2 strums an E chord with brush strokes. Learn both parts. (This example is played twice on the CD.)

NEW CHORD: E MINOR (Em)—There is only one note difference between the E and E minor chords: lift your 1st finger off the 3rd string and allow it to ring. Alternately strum the E and Em chords, and listen to the different sound quality of each.

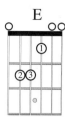

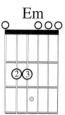

> When your hand is positioned on the neck so that your 1st finger is at the 2nd fret and your 2nd finger is at the 3rd fret and so on, you are in **2ND POSITION**.

CRIME THEME NO. 2—This is in the style of the James Bond theme.
- **Guitar 1:** The melody contrasts a line on the 5th string (B–C–C♯) against the open low E. Use the indicated left-hand fingering, which puts you in 2nd position.
- **Guitar 2:** Strum an Em chord.

BLUES BASS—This classic blues and rock bass line is used in many songs. (This example is repeated several times on the CD.)
- Memorize this pattern. Patterns like this one, which can be recalled as needed while performing, are called *riffs*.
- Play this song in 2nd position. The best way to do this is to keep your 1st finger down on the 2nd-fret B (5th string) for the entire piece.

$\frac{3}{4}$ TIME SIGNATURE

3 = Three counts per measure

4 = A quarter note receives one count

1 + 2 + 3 +

See appendix 6 for conducting pattern.

A dot next to a notehead increases the length of the note by half its value. A **DOTTED HALF NOTE** receives three beats. It is counted like three quarter notes.

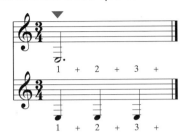

A dotted half note rhythm slash: ◇.

21

MALAGUENA MELODY—Here is a Flamenco melody in $\frac{3}{4}$. Learn it slowly, then pick up the tempo. Guitar 2 plays the chords; make sure to hold each chord for the full three counts.

Repeat 2 times

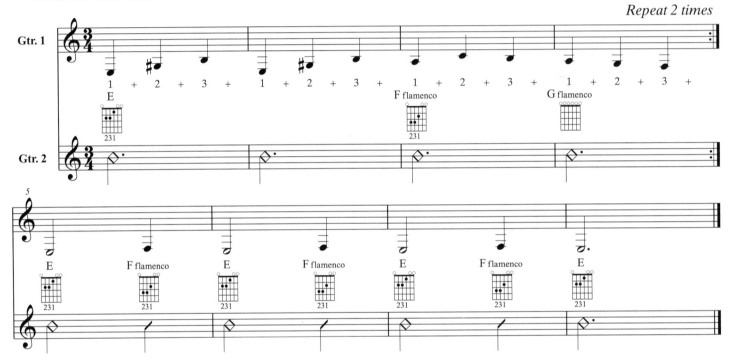

FINGERPICKING

A pick is great for strumming and playing single-note lines, but by using your right-hand thumb and fingers together, you can create beautiful **FINGERPICKING PATTERNS** as you hold simple chords with your left hand. Follow the technique instructions below.

Place your left hand in playing position, but don't fret any notes. Place the right hand as follows:

- Thumb (*p*) on the 6th string
- Index finger (*i*) on the 3rd string
- Middle finger (*m*) on the 2nd string
- Ring finger (*a*) on the 1st string

TECHNIQUE

- The thumb should sweep through the string, towards the fingers. It should touch and bounce off the tip of the index finger. Your thumb should always be in front of your fingers, not behind them.

- Each finger should push through the string.

- Each finger should remain curved and travel in an arc from the string towards the center of your palm.

- Thumb and fingers should remain relaxed and gently curved at all times. All motion should initiate from the first knuckle joint at your palm, not from bending the middle knuckle joint at the center of your finger.

THUMB AND FINGERS—Prepare by planting your thumb and fingers on the strings as indicated on the previous page.
- Pluck all four strings at the same time with your thumb and fingers—like gently closing your hand into a fist.
- Play very relaxed. Your fingers should travel in a smooth arc towards your palm, and all four notes should sound at the same time.
- The TAB indicates the strings (in this case 6, 3, 2, and 1). "Stems" have been added to the TAB in this example to indicate the rhythm, which is all quarter notes.

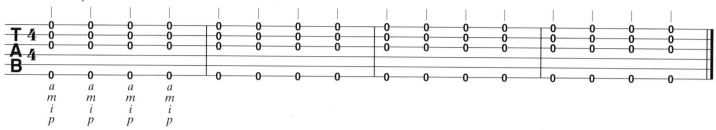

> **BLOCK CHORDS** are chords in which all tones are sounded at the same time.
> An **ARPEGGIO** is a chord in which the tones are sounded one at a time.

THUMB THEN FINGERS—In this example, you will use your thumb on beats 1–2–3–4 and your fingers on the "and" between each thumb stroke.
- Prepare to play by planting (placing in a foundational position) your thumb and fingers on the strings.
- Play the bottom string with your thumb on the count.
- On "and," close your fingers (like closing your fist) towards the palm of your hand.
- Repeat the exercise until you can play it fluidly, relaxed, and with a steady beat.

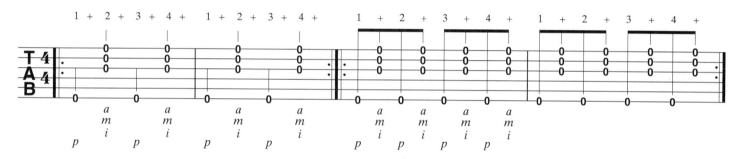

THUMB AND FINGERS SEPARATED— Perform the following example until you can play each note clearly and in rhythm.
- Prepare to play by planting your thumb and fingers on the strings.
- In this example, you will play each string separately with a different finger.
- Your thumb should sweep through the string, moving towards the tip of your index finger. Do not bend the thumb from the middle joint; it should move from the joint at the base.
- Each finger should travel in a gentle arc towards the palm of your hand. Don't bend from the middle finger joint; the movement comes from the base of each finger where it joins the palm.

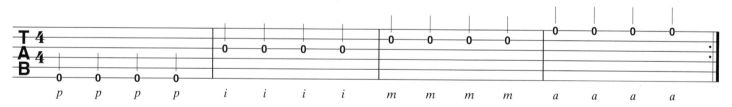

FINGERPICKING PATTERN NO. 1—This is the most common fingerpicking pattern in $\frac{4}{4}$ time. It is an eighth note pattern with the finger sequence *p–i–m–a*.
- Plant your fingers before you play. Keep a steady beat, and let the notes all ring.
- Your thumb should sweep through the string, moving towards the tip of your index finger. Do not bend the thumb from the middle finger joint.
- Each finger should travel in a gentle arc towards the palm of your hand. Again, don't bend from the middle finger joint.
- Start out slowly and play each note clearly and in rhythm.

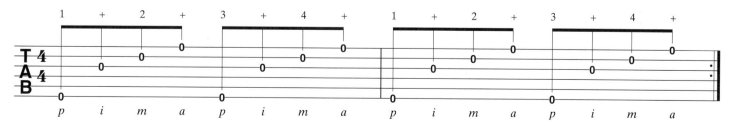

26 **FINGERPICKING IN A MINOR**—This applies the previous pattern to a chord progression.
- Prepare the right hand by placing your thumb and fingers on the strings before you play.
- The left hand will shift between Am and E. Both chords share the exact same shape and fingering. To change from Am to E and back again quickly, lift all your fingers off the strings while retaining the chord shape, then transfer the shape one string set over.

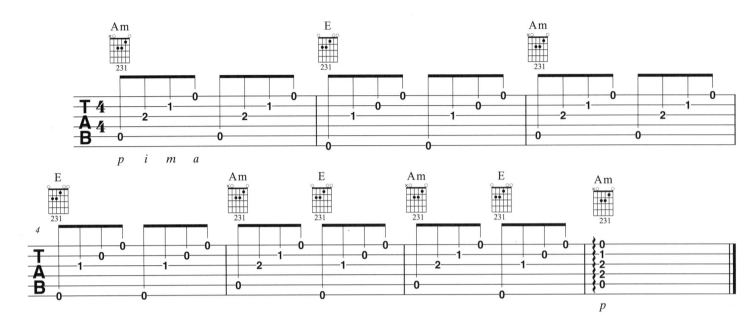

27 **GUITAR TRICKS**—As you've already seen in the Flamenco songs, a chord shape can be slid up and down the guitar neck to create beautiful and unusual chords. Interesting sounds are created by the combination of open-string notes that don't change from chord to chord and the fretted notes that do change. In the upcoming song "Acoustic Fantasy," we will take the Am chord shape and slide it up the neck to create two very unique chords: Dm/A and Bm/A.
- Dm/A: Slide the Am chord shape up to the 6th fret (one fret above the second fretboard marker). This creates a beautiful and complex-sounding chord, a type of Dm chord with an open A in the bass. It is a non-standard chord (like our "Flamenco" chords in "Flamenco Mood"), but very interesting and easy to play.
- Bm/A: Now slide the Am chord shape down to the 3rd fret (the first fretboard marker). This forms a type of Bm with an open A in the bass.
- Remember: Keep your fingers locked on the Am chord shape as you slide it up and down the strings. Don't allow your index finger to interfere with the ringing open 1st string, because that string is very important and supplies the interesting sound you hear on the recording.

TECHNIQUE TIP Lock your fingers in the Am chord shape, and focus on your index finger as you slide up and down the neck: Am is at the 1st fret, move up to the 6th fret for Dm, and move down to the 3rd fret for Bm. Strum each chord with your pick or thumb in a steady rhythm, changing to the next chord every four beats. Make sure you are getting a good, clean sound before you play "Acoustic Fantasy." (See appendix 6 for more on reading chord grids.)

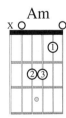 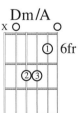 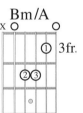

COMPOSING IDEA Experiment with moving chord shapes around the neck and see what you come up with. Many songwriter/guitarists have used this as the basis for writing new songs, and it can be a good compositional tool when writing your own songs.

When you see **1ST AND 2ND ENDINGS**, play the 1st ending, then repeat the music, skip the 1st ending, and play the 2nd ending instead.

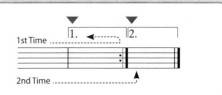

ACOUSTIC FANTASY—Here is a song based entirely on the Am chord shape.
- **Guitar 1** is the melody and is written in standard music notation.
- **Guitar 2** is a fingerstyle part using Fingerpicking Pattern No. 1 with the Am, Bm/A, and Dm/A chords. It is written in TAB only.
- As always, learn and perform both parts. Remember that you can always find a tempo where you can play the exercises without mistakes. It is okay if that is a very slow tempo—you can always increase the speed later.
- **Note:** There are many examples of songs that use moveable shapes like this. One nice example is the opening of the Allman Brothers' song "Melissa."

Acoustic Fantasy

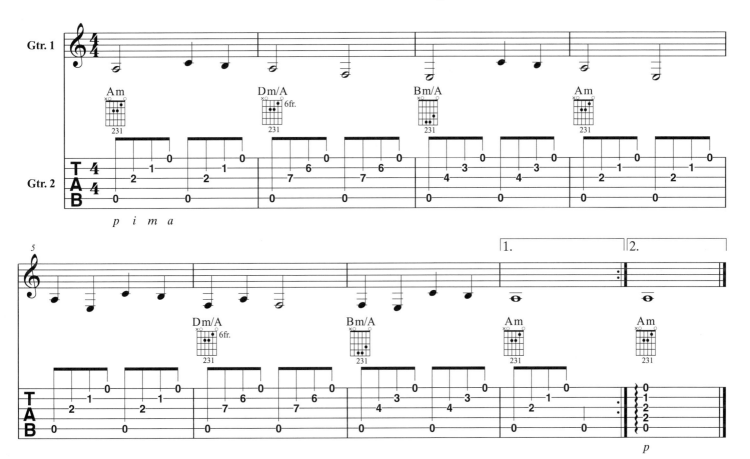

SOUND CHECK

Check off each item you can perform well.
- __ Counting and playing quarter, dotted half, half, and eighth notes
- __ Reading music on the 6th and 5th strings
- __ Using a pick
- __ Fingerpicking
- __ Following 1st and 2nd endings and repeat signs
- __ E and Am chords
- __ Playing in 1st position

Check off each item you'd like to explore further.
- __ Moving a chord shape around the neck to create interesting sounds, like F Flamenco, G Flamenco, Bm/A, and Dm/A
- __ Flamenco-style music
- __ Blues bass line riffs and crime theme melodies
- __ Music like "Acoustic Fantasy"

Level 2: Notes on the 4th and 3rd Strings

29

NEW NOTES: D, E, F, G, AND A—The notes D, E, and F are on the 4th string, and G and A are on the 3rd string.

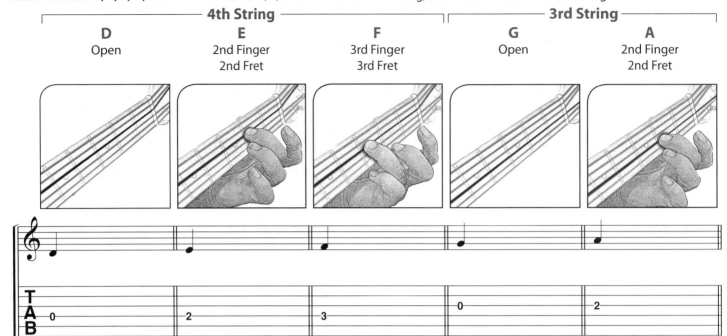

30 MORE CRIME THEME NO. 1—This is an expanded version of "Crime Theme No. 1," transposed to the D string.

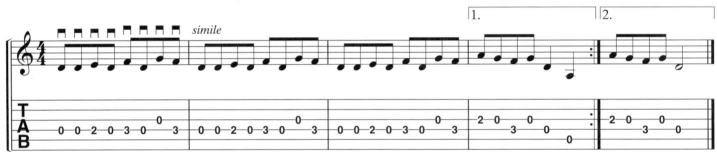

31 NEW CHORD: E7—To play an E7 chord, hold the E chord and release your 3rd finger from the 4th string, allowing the open 4th string to sound when you play the chord.

> **IMPORTANT TECHNIQUE TIP:** Arc your fingers to keep them perpendicular to the neck and do not allow them to *mute*, meaning muffle or interfere with, the open 4th string. Strum the chord and then pluck just the open 4th string to make sure it is ringing and not being stopped by your 2nd finger at the 5th string.

32 NOTE REVIEW—Remember to keep your fingers down as you ascend each string; don't lift off any note you've just played until absolutely necessary to play notes on the next string.
- **Guitar 1** plays the melody.
- **Guitar 2** plays Am and E7 chords. You can use a pick or play brush strokes with your thumb.

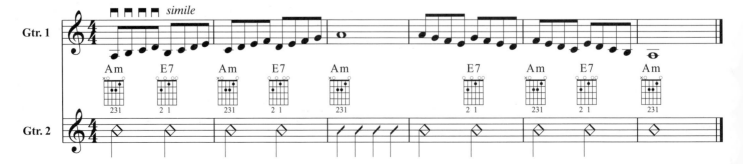

CHROMATIC notes move in **HALF STEPS**, meaning the distance is from one fret to the next. The guitar neck is constructed chromatically, meaning each fret is one half step from the neighboring fret.

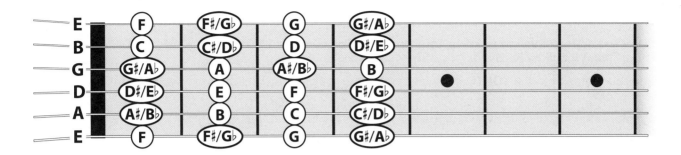

CHROMATIC STRENGTH BUILDER—This is an extended version of the exercise that we played on the 6th and 5th strings, now extended to include the 4th and 3rd strings. Keep each finger down on the string just behind the fret as you ascend. Do not lift a finger until you change strings or descend back down the pattern. This exercise is excellent for limbering up and building strength and coordination in your fingers. See appendix 4 for warm-up and stretching exercises.

Tip: It is easy to play this example by *rote*, meaning from memory, without thinking. However, if you play it slowly, looking carefully at the music and thinking about the name of each note, you will gain important insight into the logical sequence of notes on the guitar neck.

In the mid-1960s, rock artists got very serious about exploring the **BLUES** roots of rock and roll. In fact, many of the early recordings by Eric Clapton, Led Zeppelin, The Rolling Stones, and even The Beatles were actually *covers* (new versions) of songs from their favorite blues artists such as Muddy Waters, Buddy Guy, Howlin' Wolf, and Willie Dixon.

The **BLUES SONG FORM** is a very common song form in popular music. The basic blues chord progression is 12 measures long and built on just three chords: the first, fourth, and fifth chords of the song's key.

- Roman numerals are commonly used as notation for chords. The first chord in a key is I ("one"), the fourth chord is IV ("four"), and the fifth chord is V ("five").
- Count up four notes from the **TONIC** (the name of the key) to get the IV chord, and five notes from the tonic to get the V chord.
- For example, in the key of C, I is C, IV is F, and V is G. In the key of A, I is A, IV is D, and V is E.

Key of C:	**C**	D	E	**F**	**G**	A	B	C
	I	II	III	IV	V	VI	VII	I
Key of A:	**A**	B	C♯	**D**	**E**	F♯	G♯	A
	I	II	III	IV	V	VI	VII	I

34 **BLUES FORM**—Here is the basic 12-bar blues form.

As seen above, the basic 12-bar blues form follows this pattern:
- Bars 1–4: the I chord
- Bar 5: change to the IV chord
- Bar 7: return to the I chord
- Bar 9: change to the V chord
- Bar 11: return to the I chord

A common term for two-note chords consisting of just the root note and the 5th (the fifth note up the scale from the root) is **POWER CHORD**. Power chords function like big bass notes and produce a very powerful, bass-line-driven sound.

35 **THE BLUES BOOGIE PATTERN**—This pattern, which has countless variations, is the backbone of rock and blues rhythm guitar. It is based on alternation between two simple two-note chords: a power 5 chord and a power 6 chord. This example shows the chords for a blues boogie progression in the key of A, which is the most common key for guitar boogie progressions.
- Each of the following chords uses an open-string bass note.
- The upper note of each power 5 chord is played with your 1st finger.
- Do not lift your 1st finger off the string when placing your 3rd finger down to play the power 6 chords.

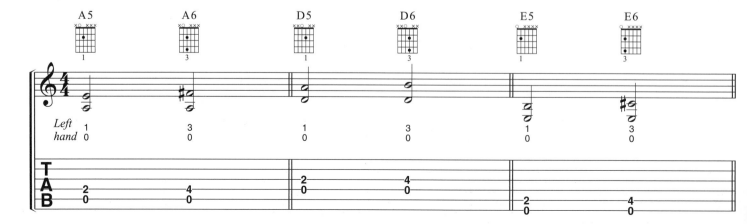

To perform a **PALM MUTE**, gently rest the palm of your picking hand against the strings just above the bridge to mute the strings—but not so hard that the notes are completely cut off. This produces a percussive sound that can be a very effective when playing boogie-type rhythm.

THE BLUES BOOGIE RHYTHM—Here is a basic 12-bar blues using the boogie pattern in the key of A.
- This type of pattern is usually played with all downstrokes, which provide a more driving rhythmic feel than down–up strokes.
- Once you are comfortable with this rhythm pattern, try using a right-hand palm mute for a more authentic rock and blues feel. Listen to the recorded example.
- Remember that, since the 1st finger of your left hand is held at the 2nd fret for this pattern, you are playing in the 2nd position.
- Don't miss the slight change in the 2nd ending. The open strings on beat 2 make a nice ending riff.

The Blues Boogie Rhythm

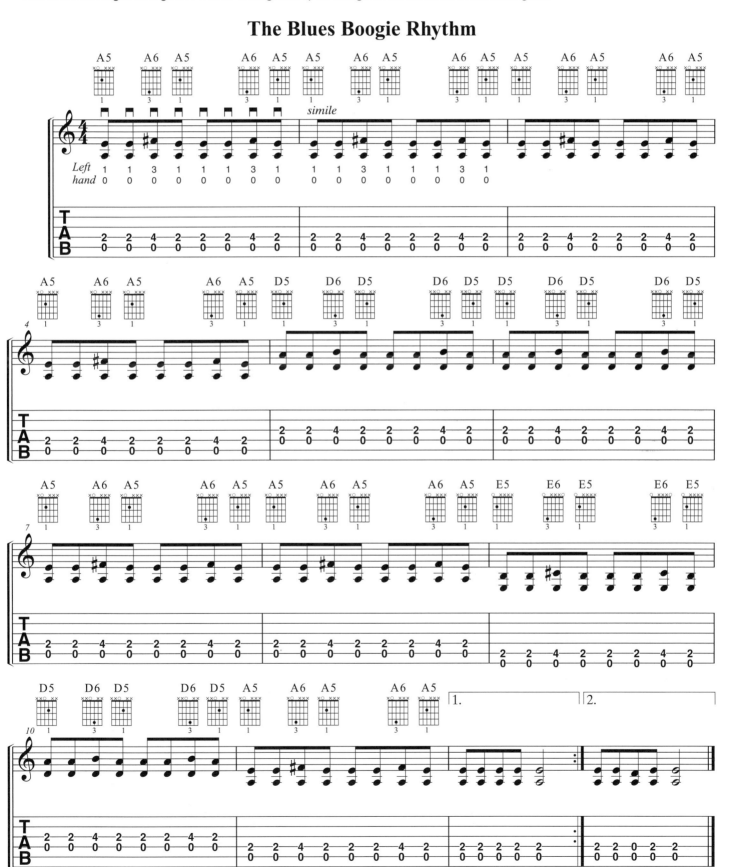

37

FINGERPICKING IN ¾—This "thumb–pluck–pluck" pattern is good preparation for using your fingers in ¾ time.
- On beat 1, sound the bass note with your thumb.
- On beats 2 and 3, sound the three-note chord with your fingers. Maintain a very steady rhythm.
- Keep your hand very relaxed—don't "pull" on the strings; just close your fingers into the palm of your hand.

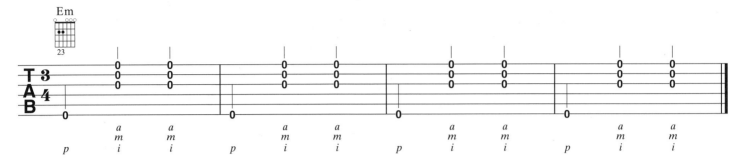

38

FINGERPICKING PATTERN NO. 2— This pattern is written in TAB only. At this point, it is not necessary to know all the notes you are playing. Just memorize the pattern so you can play it with a constant, uninterrupted rhythm.
- This is an eighth note pattern: *p–i–m–a–p–i*, counted "1 and 2 and 3 and."
- Notice that you use your thumb on beats 1 and 3.
- Listen to the CD, and try playing along with it.

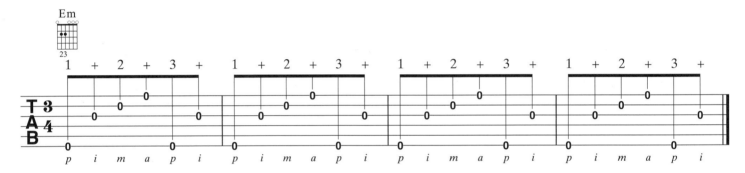

FINER POINTS OF TECHNIQUE
- Position your right hand by resting your right elbow on top of the guitar. Relax and dangle your right hand in front of the sound hole (or the pickups on an electric guitar). Now, just pivot your whole forearm so that the palm of your hand faces the strings. Keep your wrist arched, not flattened.
- All right-hand finger motion is from the first joint at your palm, not the finger joint in the middle. Push your finger through the string and straight towards the palm of your hand.
- When plucking with the *a* finger, your little finger also moves—as if they were taped together.
- Your thumb should remain straight and move from the base towards the tip of your index finger.

39

FINGERPICKING IN A MINOR ¾—Apply Fingerpicking Pattern No. 2 to the Am and E chords. Prepare the right hand by placing your thumb and fingers on the strings before you play. The left hand will shift between Am and E. Both chords have the exact same shape and fingering. Remember that, in order to quickly change from Am to E and back again, you must lift all your fingers off the strings while retaining the chord shape and transfer them over one string set.

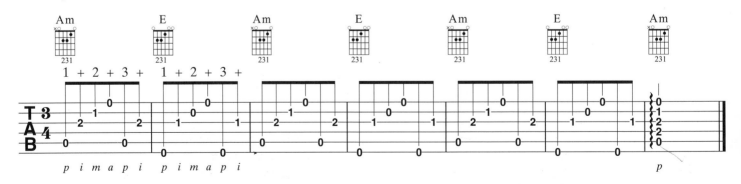

NEW CHORDS: G, C, AND D—These are three of the most commonly used guitar chords. Practice playing each one.
- The bottom note of the G chord is on string 6, the C chord on string 5 and the D chord on string 4.
- Play each chord one string at a time: Is every note clear? Fingertips need to be arched and perpendicular to the strings.
- Hold your pick loosely. Play relaxed, and you'll get a smooth and even sound.

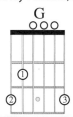
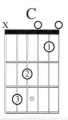
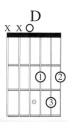

A **KEY SIGNATURE** appears at the beginning of a staff and tells you which notes are to be played sharp or flat throughout the music. A key signature with one sharp tells you that every F is played as F♯, which means you are in the **KEY OF G MAJOR**.

A **TIE** is a curved line that connects two or more notes of the same pitch. The tied notes are counted as one long note.

QUARTER REST ? = 1 count of silence.

WHOLE REST ▬ = 1 full measure of silence.

PLAISIR D'AMOUR—The melody of this French song was adapted by Elvis Presley, who recorded it as "Can't Help Falling in Love." The song begins on a pickup note. Count the first two complete beats and play on "3."

- **Guitar 1:** This is the melody. Notice the key signature and tied notes. Guitar 1 is written in standard music notation.
- **Guitar 2:** Use Fingerpicking Pattern 2 as indicated in TAB for bars 1 - 4. Apply this pattern to each chord in the song.
- **Optional Guitar 2 or 3:** Guitar 2 or a third guitar can use the basic "thumb–pluck–pluck" pattern.

Plaisir d' Amour

French Folk Song

SOUND CHECK

Check off each item you can perform well.
- __ Reading music on the 4th and 3rd strings
- __ Accidentals (sharp, flat, and natural notes)
- __ The power chords A5, A6, D5, D6, E5, and E6
- __ Em, E7, G, C, and D chords
- __ Counting a pickup measure
- __ Chromatic scales exercises

Check off each item you'd like to explore further.
- __ The blues song form
- __ Playing blues-rock rhythm guitar like "The Blues Boogie Rhythm"
- __ New fingerpicking patterns
- __ Folk and traditional music like "Plaisir d'Amour" and "Amazing Grace"
- __ Rock techniques like power chords and palm muting

Level 3: Notes on the 2nd and 1st Strings

42

NEW NOTES: B, C, D, E, F, and **G**—The notes B, C, and D are on the 2nd string, and the high E, F, and G are on the 1st string.

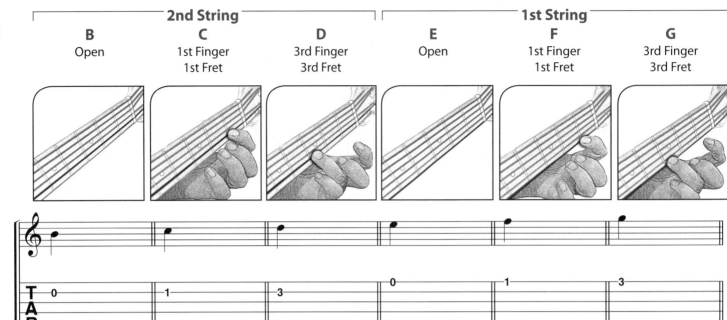

2nd String			1st String		
B	C	D	E	F	G
Open	1st Finger	3rd Finger	Open	1st Finger	3rd Finger
	1st Fret	3rd Fret		1st Fret	3rd Fret

43

NOTES ON THE 1ST AND 2ND STRINGS—Say the notes aloud as you play this example.

MELODY AND RHYTHM: In popular music, guitar is often used as a rhythm instrument to provide strummed chordal accompaniments, fingerpicked backgrounds, and driving rock riffs with power chords. The guitar is also a great melody instrument. Usually melodies are played on the higher strings of the guitar (string 4–1).

44

JINGLE BELLS—The melody for "Jingle Bells" only uses notes on the 1st and 2nd strings.

James Lord Pierpont

Jin - gle bells! Jin - gle bells! Jin - gle all the way! Oh, what fun it

is to ride a one - horse o - pen sleigh.____ one - horse o - pen sleigh.

45

WHEN THE SAINTS GO MARCHING IN—This melody is entirely on the 1st and 2nd strings.

Traditional Jazz

ALTERNATE PICKING: When playing melodies with eighth notes, it is very common to play the counts 1–2–3–4 with a downstroke (⊓) of the pick and the "ands" with an upstroke (∨). The downstroke and the upstroke are NOT two separate attacks, but one continuous motion: strike a string with a downstroke and then strike it again as your hand comes back up to playing position.

Note: Bass line-style eighth note rhythm riffs tend to be played with all downstrokes, because the downstroke provides a stronger rhythmic feel, but eighth note melodies tend to work best with alternate picking.

DOWN-UP—This example uses alternate (down-up) picking, mostly on repeated notes.

SCALE ETUDE—An *etude* is a technical study. This etude, based on the C major scale, reviews most of the notes you've learned so far and uses alternate picking on both ascending and descending eighth note lines.

For preliminary practice, try breaking the example into its four-note segments and practicing each one individually. Then, practice connecting each segment to the next until you can play the entire etude.

AMAZING GRACE (duet)—Written in 1773, this is one of the most popular melodies of all time.
- **Guitar 1** plays the melody. Use alternate picking on the eighth notes.
- **Guitar 2** provides the fingerpicked accompaniment. Use Fingerpicking Pattern No. 2.
- **Optional Guitar 3:** A third guitarist could improvise a simple strum pattern using the provided chords.

Amazing Grace

John Newton

An **ACCENT** (>) indicates to play a note or chord with a strong attack.

RIT. is an abbreviation of **RITARDANDO**, which means to gradually slow down.

49   **FLAMENCO MOOD (trio)**—Previously, we played the bass line and chords to "Flamenco Mood." Here is an expanded version of the song for three guitars. Learn each part.

Flamenco Mood

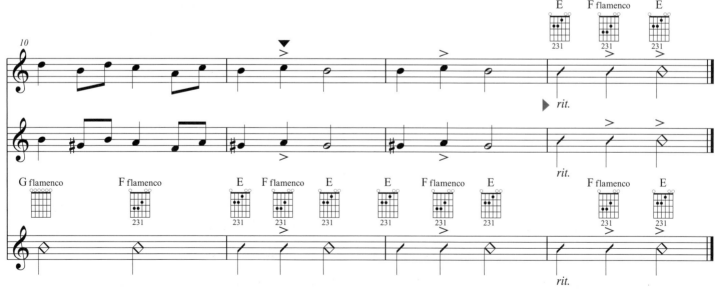

A **DOTTED QUARTER NOTE** (𝅘𝅥𝅭) receives 1½ beats, counted like three tied eighth notes or like a quarter note tied to an eighth note.

ODE TO JOY—Based on a poem (called an *Ode*) written by Freidrich Schiller in 1785, Ode to Joy is the prelude to the fourth movement of Ludwig van Beethoven's 9th symphony. By the time the symphony was first performed in Vienna on May 7, 1824, Beethoven was totally deaf; however, he could write the music he heard in his head, even though he could not hear it with his ears!

- **Guitar 1** plays the melody. Use alternate picking on the eighth notes.
- **Guitar 2** plays a harmony part. Harmony is created when two or more musical tones are sounded at the same time. This harmony part moves parallel with the melody. (Note: The C♯ in bar 12 is played at the 4th fret of the 5th string.)
- **Guitar 3** plays the accompaniment using Fingerpicking Pattern No. 1. Guitar 3 is written in TAB only. Follow the TAB, or simply apply the memorized pattern to the chords indicated above the music.
- **Optional Guitar 3 or 4:** Instead of playing the fingerpicking pattern, improvise a simple strumming rhythm (begin with quarter notes). Optionally, a fourth guitar can strum while the third guitar fingerpicks.

Ode to Joy

Ludwig Van Beethoven

51 **CHROMATIC STRENGTH BUILDER**—This exercise uses all six strings.
- **Note:** On the guitar, the exact same note can often be played on different strings at different frets. For example, there is an open B on the 2nd string, and there is also a fretted B on the 3rd string at the 4th fret.
- **Remember:** Chromatic notes move in half steps. As you ascend from note to note, keep each finger down on the fret. Do not lift a finger until you change strings or descend back down the pattern.
- **Tip:** It is easy to play this example from memory, without thinking; however, if you play it slowly while carefully looking at the music and thinking about the name of each note, you will gain important insight into the logical sequence of notes on the guitar neck.

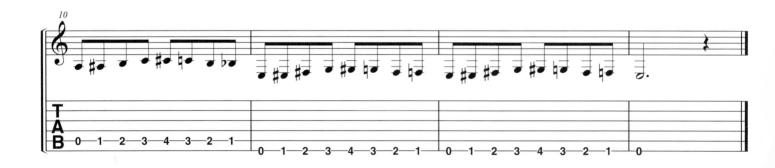

To **IMPROVISE** means to create music as you play. Think of it as the spontaneous reorganization of what you already know into new, unplanned variations.

A **LICK** is a pre-learned pattern that you can use as you improvise a guitar solo, inserting it wherever it seems appropriate. The following **BLUES LICKS** can be played over a blues progression in the key of A.

THE ONE-GRIP BLUES PATTERN—This is an example of a classic blues lick. We will use the same two-finger chord *grip* (left-hand fingering arrangement) for each of the three chords in the blues progression as shown below.
- For the I chord (A7), the grip is at the 2nd fret.
- For the IV chord (D7), slide the grip down one fret to the 1st fret.
- For the V chord (E7), slide the grip up to the 3rd fret.
- Play with a strong rhythm using all downstrokes as indicated.

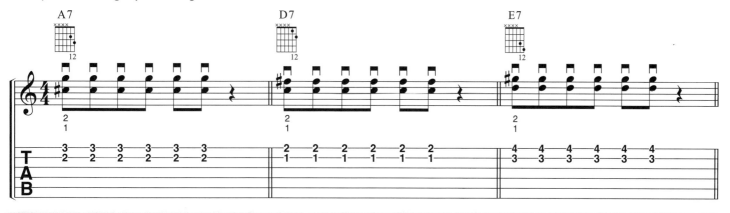

HAMMER-ON: Play the first note, then "hammer" your finger down with enough force to sound the next note.

SLIDE: Play the first note, then slide with enough force to sound the next note. Do not strike the second note.

ADVANCED OPTIONAL LEAD GUITAR VARIATION—If you can play the above licks with complete confidence and are looking for a challenge, try this advanced variation. First, place your hand in the two-finger grip position on the first two strings. As you play these licks, your hand should always stay fixed in the grip position.
- For the A chord, play the 1st-fret C with your 1st finger. Strike the note, and then *slide* up to the 2nd-fret C♯. Do not strike the C♯ again; it should be sounded by the force of your finger sliding up from C. Then play the 1st-string G with your 2nd finger.
- For the D chord, play the open B, and then *hammer* your 1st finger down onto the C with enough force to sound the note. Then play the F♯ with your 2nd finger.
- For the E chord, start on the 2nd-fret C♯, and slide up exactly as you did for the A chord.

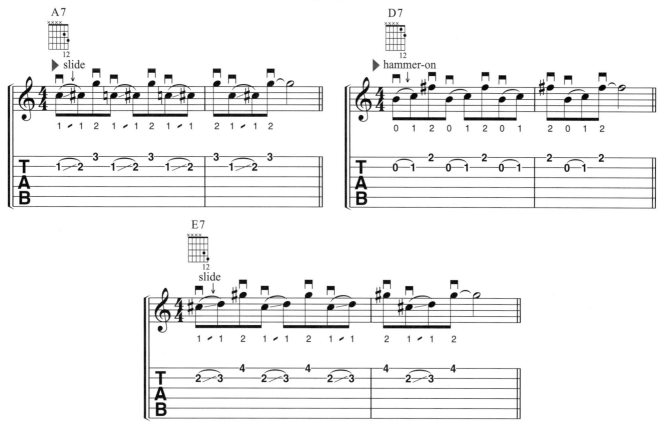

54 **ONE-GRIP BLUES**—The rhythm part to this song is based on the blues progression you learned earlier. The lead guitar part is based on the two-finger grip you learned in the previous example.

- The song starts with a classic blues introduction. Memorize this pattern. You can use it to start off any blues in the key of A whenever you jam with others.
- Measures 13 and 14 (1st ending) feature a classic blues *turnaround*, which comes at the end of the 12-bar blues progression and sets it up to repeat. The turnaround is a two-bar melody that makes the music feel like it isn't done, but instead turns it around to begin the progression again.
- Measures 13 and 15 (2nd ending) use the same turnaround lick, but it is altered in a way that signals an ending to the song instead of a return to the beginning.
- Chord frames are not indicated throughout the rhythm guitar part. Typically, just the basic names of the chords (A7, D7, and E7) are indicated, and it's assumed the guitarist just knows to play the boogie pattern or one of its many variations.
- Notice that, even though the names of the chords do not appear to be close to each other, the grip moves just one fret down for the IV chord and just one fret up for the V chord.
- On the recording, the lead guitarist improvises a solo on the repeat based on the optional slide and hammer licks learned on the previous page. Once you are comfortable playing the entire song, you may want to experiment with improvising your own blues solos over the recorded rhythm of track 55 as described on the next page.

One-Grip Blues

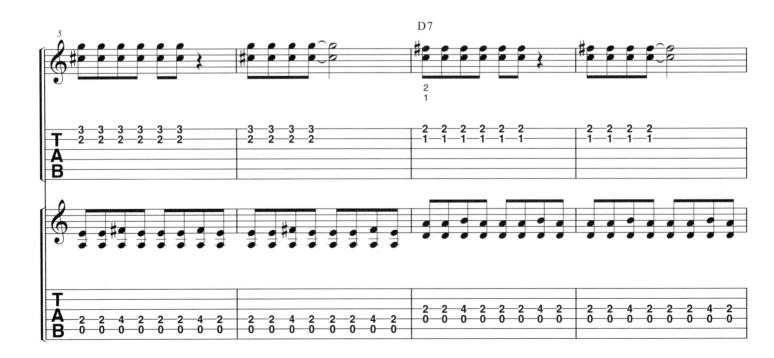

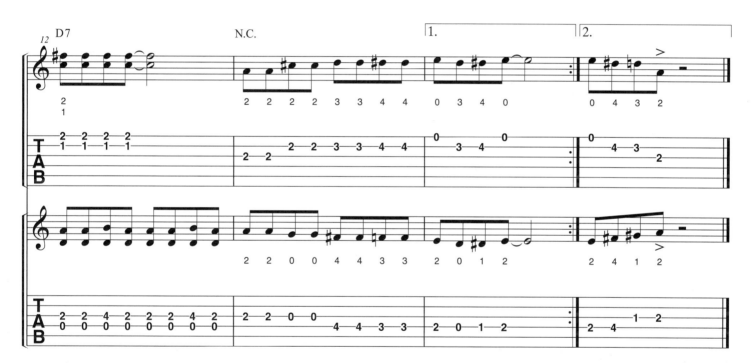

IMPROVISATION AND BLUES SOLOING ON ONE-GRIP BLUES—Track 55 is just the rhythm track for "One-Grip Blues." Use it to practice improvising your own solos. Use both the basic one-grip riff and the optional lead variations. Make sure you carefully play only "A" riffs over the A chords, "D" riffs over the D chords, and "E" riffs over the E chords.

SOUND CHECK

Check off each item you can perform well.
___ Reading music on the 2nd and 1st strings
___ Dotted quarter notes
___ Alternate picking
___ Ritardando *(rit.)*
___ Accents

Check off each item you'd like to explore further.
___ Flamenco music like "Flamenco Mood"
___ Classical music like "Ode to Joy"
___ Blues-rock and blues licks such as "One-Grip Blues"
___ Improvisation using licks

Level 4: Chords, Music Theory, and Playing by Ear

A **CHORD** consists of three or more notes played at the same time.

CHORD SYMBOLS identify the names of chords.

MAJOR chords are simply identified with the letter name of the chord, which you've learned is called the *root*. For example, the chord symbol C indicates a C major chord.

MINOR chords are identified with the root plus an "m" for "minor." For example, the chord symbol for C minor is Cm.

DOMINANT 7TH chords are identified by the root of the chord plus the number 7. For example, the chord symbol for a G dominant 7th chord is G7.

Note: Major, minor, and dominant 7th are the three basic chord families. All chords fit into one of these three families. As you play them, you will hear that each type has a very different, characteristic sound.

Notice how similar the C and G7 chord shapes are. When changing chords, make an effort to visualize the next chord before making the change. To change from C to G7, just spread out your fingering by moving all three fingers simultaneously, not one at a time: your 1st finger shifts from the 2nd string to the 1st string, your 2nd finger shifts from the 4th string to the 5th string, and your 3rd finger shifts from the 5th string to the 6th string.

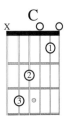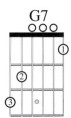

56 **C TO G7**—Practice changing chords smoothly.

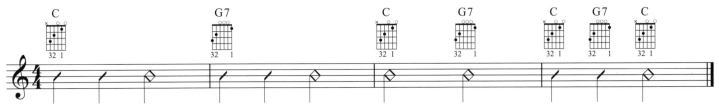

57 **C TO G7, FINGERSTYLE**
- **Guitar 1** plays a simple alternate picked melody. This part is written in standard music notation.
- **Guitar 2** will use Fingerpicking Pattern No. 1 over the C and G7 chords. This part is written in TAB only.
- **Optional Guitar 2** or a third guitar can play the chords using the "thumb–pluck–thumb–pluck" pattern.

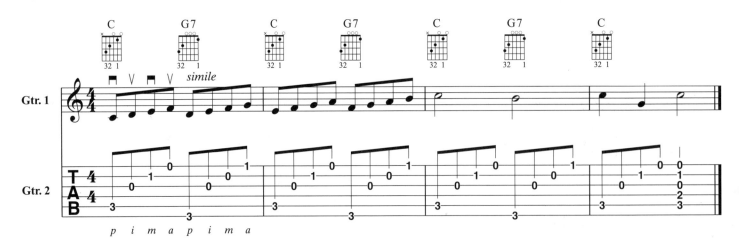

KEY OF C—Here is a C major scale.

C	D	E	F	G	A	B	C

- Your teacher will play a C chord. Listen to the chord and sing the C scale.

Do	Re	Mi	Fa	Sol	La	Ti	Do

- The C chord (C–E–G) is built on the first note of the scale. The G7 chord (G–B–D–F) is built on the fifth note of the scale.

C	D	E	F	**G**	A	B	C
1	2	3	4	**5**	6	7	1

- Your teacher will play a C chord. Listen to the chord and sing the root (C) and the 5th (G). You can sing syllables "Do–Sol–Do" or numbers "1–5–1."

- **Review:** Chords are identified with Roman numerals. In the key of C, the C chord is the I chord and the G chord is the V chord.

C	D	E	F	**G**	A	B	**C**
I				**V**			**I**

> Being able to identify the sound of changing notes, chords, and other musical elements is a very useful skill. Knowing how to play a song based on how it should sound is called **PLAYING BY EAR**.

HE'S GOT THE WHOLE WORLD IN HIS HANDS—This song uses just two chords: the I chord (C) and the V7 chord (G7). In the following arrangement, only the starting chord is given. You will figure out the rest of the chords using one of these methods:

1. Begin on the C chord and sing the song to yourself. Stop when the chord seems to clash or sound bad with the melody. Do this several times until you can identify the exact word or syllable where the chord began to clash, and that is where you change to G7. Continue this process throughout the song, remembering that the correct chord will always be either C or G7. Write the chord symbols above the words.
2. Your teacher will strum and sing the song, staying on just the C chord until the class identifies when to change chords based on the clash described above.
3. First, listen to the song on the CD with the guitar accompaniment, then play along with the 2nd version (track 60, minus guitar), and let your ear guide the change from C to G7 and back again.

HE'S GOT THE WHOLE WORLD IN HIS HANDS (minus guitar)—Write in the chords above the words. The first chord (C) is provided for you.

Starting pitch: **G**

Verses 1 and 3:

      C
He's got the whole world in His hands,

He's got the whole world in His hands,

He's got the whole world in His hands,

He's got the whole world in His hands.

Verse 2:

He's got the itty-bitty baby in His hands,

He's got the itty-bitty baby in His hands,

He's got the itty-bitty baby in His hands,

He's got the whole world in His hands.

TWO-CHORD SONGS

The following songs use only the I and V7 chords. Pick one you know, and try to sing the melody while accompanying yourself on the guitar. Make up your own strum pattern, and use your ear to figure out when to change chords.

Down in the Valley	Merrily, We Roll Along
Jambalaya	Polly Wolly Doodle
My Darlin' Clementine	Shoo Fly, Don't Bother Me
Farmer in the Dell	Three Blind Mice
Mary Had a Little Lamb	

30

MUSICAL ROAD MAPS

A **CODA** (✛) is the ending of a song.

D.S. AL CODA means to jump back to the sign 𝄋 and play until you reach the *To Coda* ✛ indication.

TO CODA ✛ means to jump to the coda.

61 **SIMPLE GIFTS**—This shaker tune was written in 1848, and its beautiful melody is so popular that it has been used in compositions ranging from those of the great American classical composer Aaron Copland (in both "Appalachian Spring" and "Old American Songs") all the way to the rock band Weezer ("The Greatest Man That Ever Lived"). In this arrangement, the rhythm guitar can play either the fingerpicking pattern or the strum. If you have three guitars, try all three parts together.

- **Guitar 1:** This is the melody. Play it with a pick and use standard alternate picking on the eighth notes. Play it smooth and pretty.
- **Guitar 2:** This fingerpicking accompaniment applies just the basic $\frac{4}{4}$ fingerpicking pattern to each of the song's two chords (G and D).
- **Guitar 3:** This is a strum-style accompaniment. Hold the pick loosely and swing from your wrist. Remember, on the upstroke of the strum, your pick travels in an upward arc, usually only striking the top three or four strings.

Simple Gifts

Lyrics by Elder Joseph
Music by Joseph Brackett

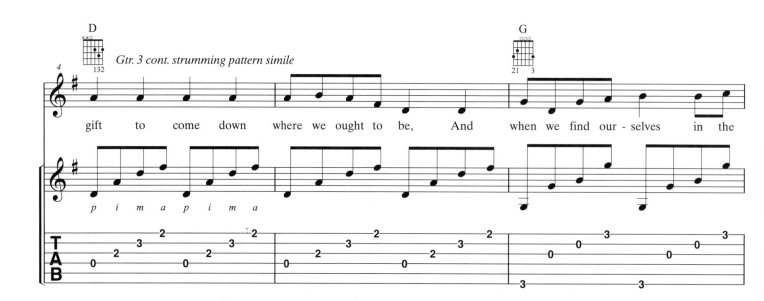

As you learned earlier, *ritardando* means the tempo should become gradually slower. It is often indicated with the abbreviation *rit.* **A TEMPO** means to resume the original tempo.

62

FÜR ELISE (duet)—Here is a guitar duet based on one of Beethoven's most popular piano pieces, which has been arranged for many different solo instruments and ensembles.

- **Guitar 1:** This is the song's melody. Use your 4th finger for the 2nd string D♯, and count very carefully. Guitar 1 is written in standard notation.
- **Guitar 2:** This is a ¾ accompaniment part built from the standard guitar chords Am, E7, C, and G. It is a nice example that demonstrates how even classical music can be broken down into a basic melody and chord progression. The G/B chord in measure 12 (called a slash chord because the slash indicates a different bass note other than the usual root tone) is a partial voicing of the basic G chord with just the middle four strings. Using the B as the bottom note creates a nice bass line leading from C down to A. Guitar 2 is written in Tablature only.
- **Optional Guitar 3:** Improvise a fingerpicking accompaniment based on Fingerpicking Pattern 2.
- **Note:** Developing mental pictures of chord fingerings, as shown in chord frame diagrams, will help you remember the correct fingerings and develop accompaniment parts when music only contains a melody and chord symbols.

Für Elise

Ludwig van Beethoven

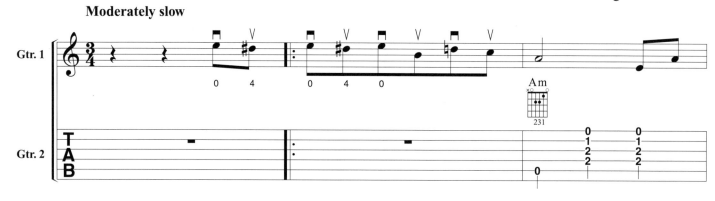

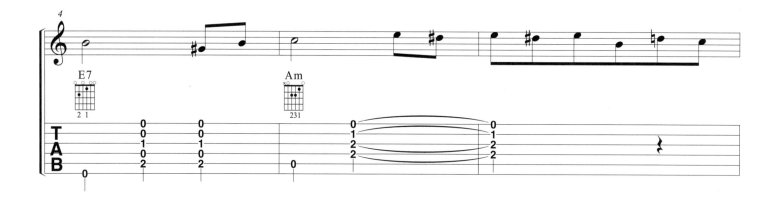

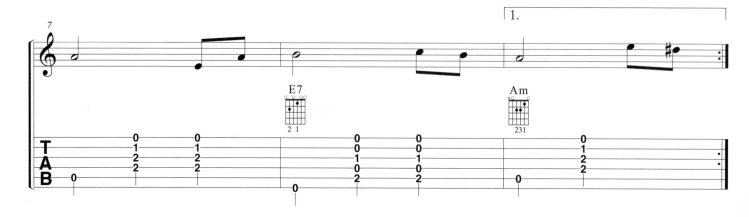

It is often said that jazz music "swings." Early jazz set itself apart from folk and classical music by interpreting eighth notes with a **SWING FEEL**, which means they are played in uneven, long-short pairs called **SWING** eighths, instead of normal, even **STRAIGHT** eighth pairs. An indication is usually placed at the beginning of a song to tell you to play the eighth notes swing style.

63 **SWING EXAMPLE NO. 1**—You will hear this example played with straight eighth notes (even) and then with swing eighth notes (uneven, long-short). Play along with the CD until you are comfortable playing the swing eighth notes. They are written exactly like straight eighth notes, but interpreted as a long-short rhythm, like a gallop. Use the syllable "uh" instead of "and" as indicated below for counting swing eighths.

Straight eighth notes are played evenly: Swing eighth notes are played long-short (gallop):

64 **SWING EXAMPLE NO. 2**—Here is the opening phrase of "When the Saints Go Marching In," interpreted as a Dixieland jazz musician might, with a swing-style eighth note melody.

Swing feel

A **STACCATO** dot above or below a note (♩˙ ˙♩) means to cut a note short by not letting it ring. A staccato with an accent (♩˙ ˙♩) means to play the note staccato and accented.

The use of **BLUE NOTES**, which come from blues music, is something that sets jazz apart from folk and classical styles. These dissonant notes were originally used by early blues singers to bring a "grittier" feel to the music.

65 **WHEN THE SAINTS GO MARCHIN' IN (duet)**—We've already used blue notes in previous blues bass line examples, and the second guitar part to this arrangement uses the blue notes B♭ and F♮.

- **Guitar 1** is a jazz-style version of the traditional melody.
- **Guitar 2** is the harmony part. Some is traditional parallel harmony that simply follows along with the melody (see measures 6–7 and 11–13), and some is counter-melody—a part that fills in the spaces between the melody phrases (see measures 2–5 and 8–9). Look for the blue notes in the counter-melody and remember to play this with a swing feel. In measure 8, try moving to 2nd position so you can play with your 2nd and 3rd fingers.
- **Guitar 3** plays the chords using a quarter note strum rhythm. To sound like a jazz rhythm player, play each chord staccato (don't let it ring), and accent beats 2 and 4.

When the Saints Go Marchin' In

Traditional Jazz

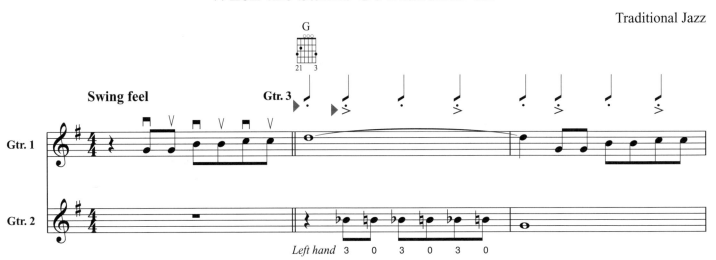

Left hand 3 0 3 0 3 0

SOUND CHECK

Check off each item you can perform well.
__ Staccato
__ Following the form indications ***D.S. al Coda*** and ***To Coda***
__ Playing jazz with a swing feel

Check off each item you'd like to explore further.
__ Playing "by ear"
__ Exploring music theory by learning how chords and scales are created
__ Traditional music like "Simple Gifts"
__ Classical music like "Für Elise"
__ Jazz music like "When the Saints Go Marchin' In"

Level 5: Three-Chord Rock and Blues

THREE-CHORD ROCK AND ROLL

Like the blues progression, many rock songs are based on just the I, IV, and V chords. The following common three-chord rock and roll chord pattern is found in countless songs including, "Wild Thing," "Hang On Sloopy," "Twist and Shout," "Louie, Louie," "La Bamba," "Get Off of My Cloud," "Good Lovin'," "Love Is All Around," and "You've Lost That Lovin' Feeling."

Tip: It's important to understand that all songs have many things in common, so whenever you learn a chord progression or standard rhythm pattern for one song, you are actually learning something that will apply to many, many other songs you play.

KEY SIGNATURES

1 sharp (F#) = Key of G 　　　2 sharps (F#, C#) = Key of D

3 sharps (F#, C#, G#) = Key of A

An eighth rest equals an eighth note: 𝄾 = ♪

66 **THREE-CHORD ROCK AND ROLL IN G**—This progression is excellent practice for learning to change chords in tempo.

67 **THREE-CHORD ROCK AND ROLL IN D**—This example introduces an A chord. Use the indicated fingering.

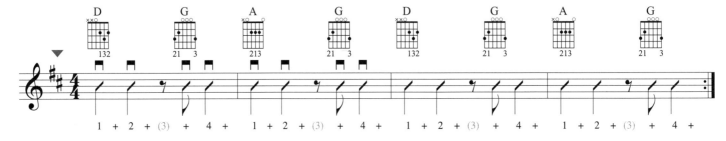

68 **THREE-CHORD ROCK AND ROLL IN A**—Here is the same common progression in the key of A. Sometimes there are common fingers when changing from one chord to another. Look for those and use the same fingers wherever possible.
- When playing the A chord, your 1st finger is on the 3rd string. Don't lift it as you change to the D chord.
- As you change from the D chord to the E chord, you can keep your 1st finger on the string, but slide it backwards one fret so it is in position to play the E chord. Then, place your 2nd and 3rd fingers down.

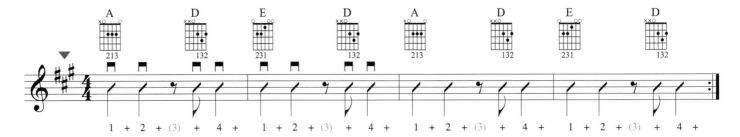

ALTERNATING THUMB-PLUCK PATTERN—This is a critically important rhythm pattern. When mastered, it will open the door to thousands of great fingerpicking patterns.
- On beats 1 and 3, your thumb plays the bass note.
- On beats 2 and 4, pluck the middle three-string chord with your thumb, index, and middle fingers. This means your thumb will constantly alternate between the bass note and the 4th string.

First, get used to the alternating thumb:

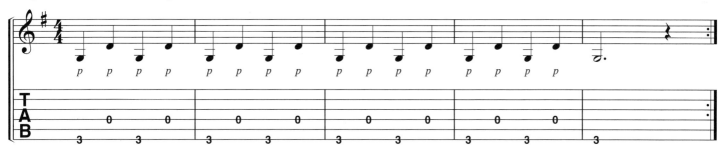

Now add the chords as shown here:

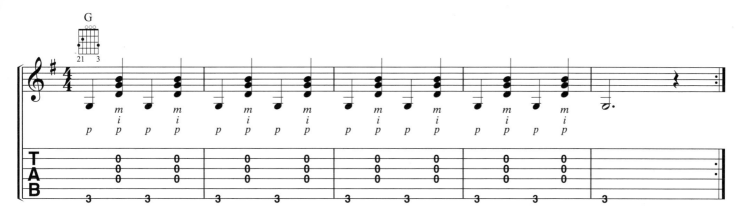

"Corinna, Corinna," which you will find on the next page, is a great example of traditional American **ROOTS MUSIC.** Roots music refers to the uniquely American melting pot of various types of ethnic and regional folk music that eventually coalesced into modern popular music such as rock, jazz, and country. Two of the main branches of American roots music are "old time" mountain music and blues.

Blues songs often use the **SHUFFLE** rhythm, which means the eighth notes are uneven, exactly like the jazz swing rhythm. One of the main differences between shuffle and swing tunes is that the bass player plays a constant quarter note walking bass line, while shuffle tunes tend to be slower with no walking bass.

CORINNA, CORINNA—This song is a classic example of early American blues. Look for recorded examples on iTunes, especially by early blues musicians like Blind Lemon Jefferson.
- **Guitar 1:** This is the melody. Use a shuffle rhythm on the eighth notes.
- **Guitar 2:** This is the accompaniment and uses the "thumb–pluck–thumb–pluck" pattern. Measure 11 introduces the D/F# chord. Carefully follow the fingering diagram

Corinna, Corinna

Traditional Blues

Sightreading II

Guitar

Rhythms

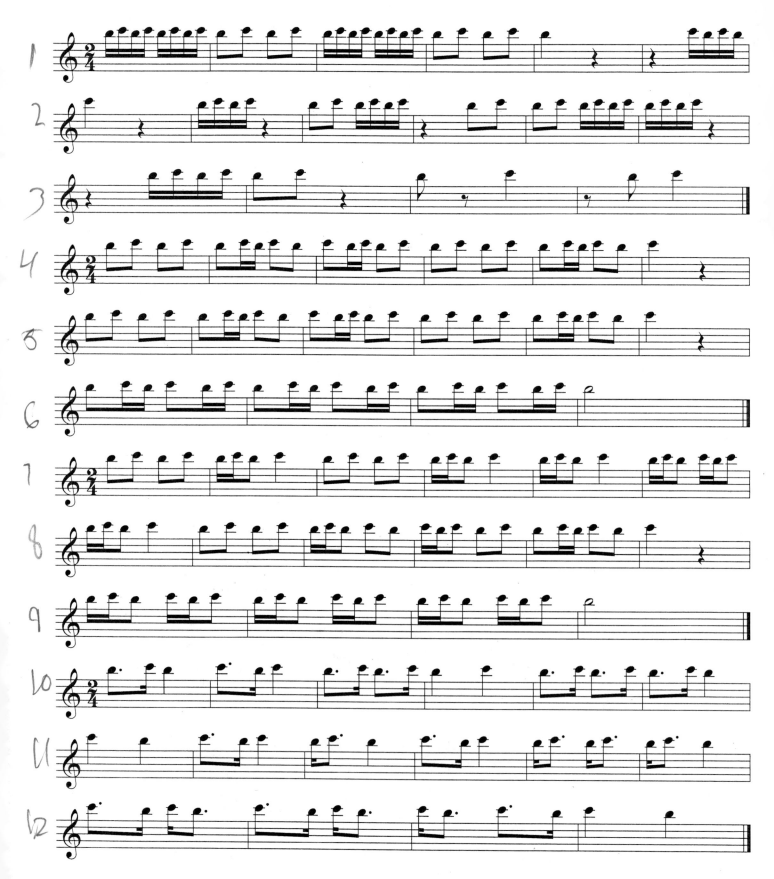

NEW CHORDS: A7 AND D7—These chords are needed to play a blues song in the key of A.

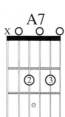

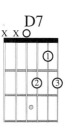

The single most common three-chord pattern in popular music is the **BLUES PROGRESSION**. As you learned earlier, the blues is a 12-bar song form that only uses the I, IV, and V chords.

A BLUES SHUFFLE—This blues progression in the key of A uses a shuffle rhythm (uneven eighth notes).
- This is a bass-line-style riff played in 2nd position. Follow the left-hand fingerings carefully.
- The riff pattern is always the same. Just move it to the correct string set as shown in the TAB.
- Listen to the recording to get a feel for the rhythm.
- This riff is played with a pick, preferably using all downstrokes.
- An optional rhythm guitar part can be improvised based on the chord symbols. Start with an eighth note shuffle strum.

A Blues Shuffle

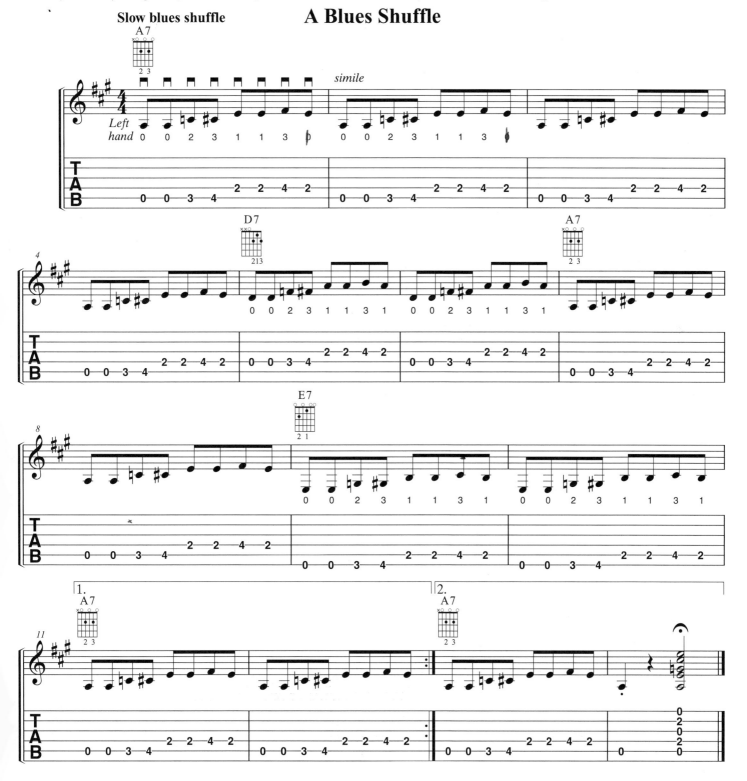

40

Holding down two or more strings with one finger is called a **BARRE**. Because barre chords often have no open strings, they are **MOVEABLE** chords, meaning you can take the shape and slide it to another fret for a different chord. If, at first, the barre is difficult to execute, move the shape to a higher fret such as the 5th or 7th fret where the strings are easier to press down, and work towards bringing the shape towards the nut until you can play it with clear notes.

73

NEW CHORD: F—The F chord is challenging for some beginners because it uses a two-string barre. Here's how to play it.
1. Place your 3rd finger at the 3rd fret on the 4th string.
2. Place your 2nd finger at the 2nd fret on the 3rd string.
3. Now lay your 1st finger flat across the 1st and 2nd strings at the 1st fret for the barre. Try to get a clear sound from all four strings, but if you can't, just make sure strings 4, 3, and 2 are clear, and eventually you'll get the 1st string also.

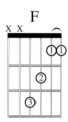

74

F BARRE CHORD ETUDE—Because the F barre chord has no open strings, it is a *moveable* chord form: it is an F chord at the 1st fret, an F♯ chord at the 2nd fret, a G chord at the 3rd fret, and so on. In this case, the root of the chord is the top note, played on the 1st string. This chord etude shows how the chord can be moved up and down the neck. It actually gets easier, not harder, to play as you move up the neck.

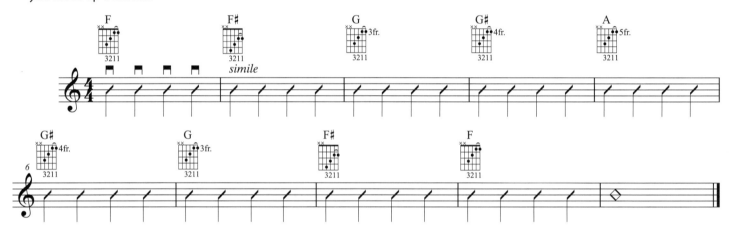

75

BARRE CHORDS BY THE BAY—This chord progression is in the style of Otis Redding's classic "Sittin' on the Dock of the Bay." It uses just the F chord form, moving up and down the neck.

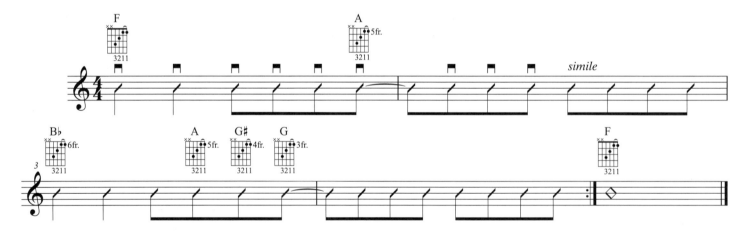

▶ **SOUND CHECK**

Check off each item you can perform well.
__ Alternating thumb-pluck pattern
__ Shuffle rhythm
__ The moveable F barre chord form

Check off each item you'd like to explore further.
__ Three-chord rock and roll patterns
__ Folk and traditional blues music like "Corinna, Corinna"
__ Shuffle blues like the "A Blues Shuffle"

Level 6: Songs and Repertoire

DYNAMICS indicate changes in volume that add interest and emotional appeal to a performance.

FORTE (*f*) indicates to play loud.

MEZZO FORTE (*mf*) indicates to play medium loud. Pressure from your thumb pushes the pick through the string. The harder your thumb pushes the pick, the louder the note will be.

PIANO (*p*) indicates to play softly. Use a gentle hand motion with minimal force from your thumb.

MEZZO PIANO (*mp*) indicates to play medium soft.

MINUET IN G—Here is a guitar ensemble arrangement of "Minuet in G" from Johann Sebastian Bach's *Notebook for Anna Magdalena*. The I, IV, and V chords are the most important chords in any key. Here, you can see that even Bach based some of his songs on just those three chords.

- **Guitar 1** plays the melody.
- **Guitar 2** is an interesting eighth note rhythmic part played entirely on the 3rd and 4th strings, constantly alternating between them. Strict alternate picking is suggested, but all downstrokes will work, too.
- **Guitar 3** is the rhythm guitar. Experiment with adding some eighth note strums once the rhythm is solid.
- **Optional Guitar 3 or 4:** Play the chords using Fingerpicking Pattern No. 2.

Minuet in G

J.S. Bach

42

77 **NEW CHORDS:** Dm—When changing from A7 to Dm use your 2nd finger as a guide. Position it first and allow the other fingers to follow.

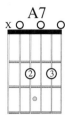

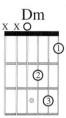

78 **AGUADO STUDY**—This beautiful melody by classical guitar composer Dionisio Aguado is arranged here for two guitars with an optional third guitar.
- **Guitar 1** is the melody, played entirely as arpeggios (chord tones played individually) on the top three strings. Hold the fingers as indicated to allow all the notes to ring until you change to the next measure. The melody for the E7 chord is in 3rd position (1st finger at the 3rd fret). **Note:** This part can be played fingerstyle (*p–i–m–i–p–i–m–i*), or it can be played pickstyle using either strict alternate picking or the glide picking pattern shown above the music (⊓ ⊓ ⊓ V).
- **Guitar 2** plays the bass line.
- **Optional Guitar 3** strums the indicated chords. Be sure not to overpower the other guitars.

Aguado Study

Dionisio Aguado

A grouping of three eighth notes in one beat is called a **TRIPLET**: In shuffle and swing feels, the basic quarter note can be subdivided into either two eighth notes played long-short, or into three equal parts.

TRIPLET EXAMPLE NO. 1—This example shows how triplets are counted. Listen to the recording.

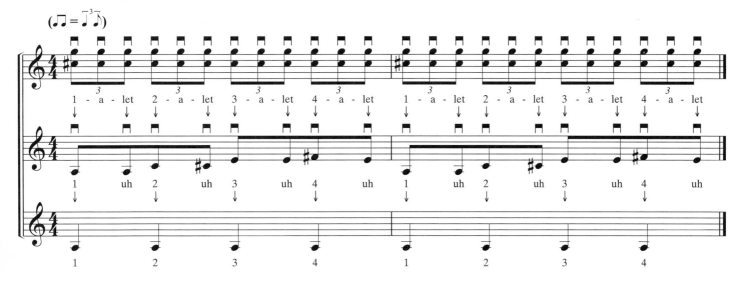

TRIPLET EXAMPLE NO. 2—This example shows how the shuffle eighth notes line up with triplets.

ONE-FINGER BLUES RIFF—This is a classic blues riff.
- **For the A7 riff:** Barre the top three strings at the 2nd fret with your 1st finger. Play the chord, then release and play the three open strings.
- **For the D7 riff:** Barre the top three strings at the 7th fret with your 1st finger. Play the chord, then quickly slide the 1st finger barre down two frets to the 5th fret. The slide should be strong enough to sound the chord without using your pick again. If you don't have the strength for the slide yet, just move down two frets and strike the strings again.
- **For the E7 riff:** Barre the top three strings at the 9th fret with your 1st finger. Play the chord, then slide down to the 7th fret as you did for the D riff. Again, if you don't have the strength for the slide yet, just move down two frets and strike the strings again.

82 **ONE-FINGER BLUES**—This song is a shuffle blues combining three classic patterns.

- **Guitar 1** plays the classic blues rhythm riff taught in line 68. This part is written in notation and TAB to help you visualize and locate the chord fingerings for the D7 and E7 patterns.
- **Guitar 2** is the "A Blues Shuffle" line that you played in line 72. It is shown in standard notation only.
- **Guitar 3** plays the "One Grip Blues Pattern" from line 52 on the repeat (don't play the first time through). This part is written in standard music notation only.

One Finger Blues

83 **ROMANZA**—This is one of the most popular and beautiful melodies in the classical guitar repertoire. It is usually performed as a guitar solo, but is arranged here for three guitars.

- **Guitar 1:** This is the melody, played with a pick. Listen carefully to the recording.
- **Guitar 2:** This is the accompaniment part. Hold the indicated chords and use the ¾ "thumb–pluck–pluck" pattern. To use a pick instead, play the indicated bass note, then strum the rest of the chord with the pick in a "bass–strum–strum" pattern.
- **Guitar 3:** This is where the really fun stuff is. The entire part is played on strings 5–4–3 using the indicated chord fingerings. Don't worry about the names of the Em9 and Am6 chords—they sound complicated, but are easy to play. Notice how they add a very dark, mysterious quality to the song. The fingerpicking pattern is a strict alternating thumb pattern: *p–i–p–i–p–i*. Note that this pattern can also be easily played with a pick; all downstrokes are recommended, but alternate picking works very well, too.
- **New Chord:** This song introduces the B7 chord (measure 11). Follow the fingering diagram carefully. Practice playing the chord before you try to play it as part of the song.

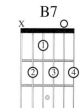

Romanza

Moderately fast

Spanish Folk Song

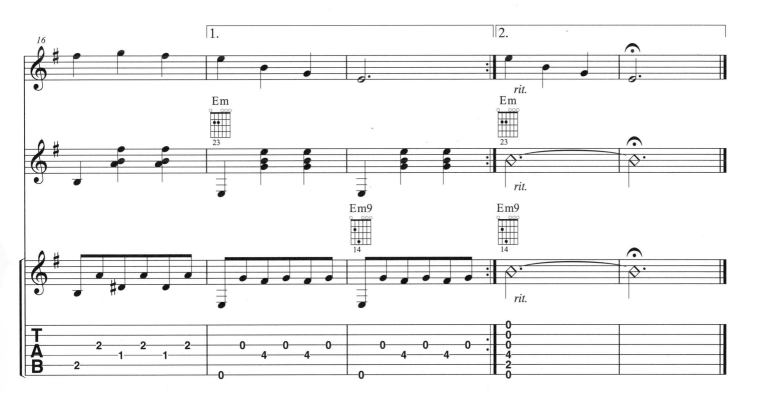

84

SIMPLE GIFTS (solo)—You learned "Simple Gifts" previously. Here is an arrangement of this beautiful melody for solo guitar.
- In between the melody notes, open strings are used to fill out the sound. Let all notes rings as long as possible.
- **Technique:** Allow melody notes to ring while playing the open-string filler notes. For example, in measure 2, hold the 3rd-fret D while playing open G; in measure 3, hold the 2nd-fret A while playing open D.

Simple Gifts

Traditional

▶ **SOUND CHECK**

Check off each item you can perform well.
- __ Triplet rhythm
- __ Dynamics
- __ A7 and Dm chords

Check off each item you'd like to explore further.
- __ Classical music like Bach's "Minuet in G" or "Aguado Study"
- __ Rock and blues riffs like the "One-Finger Blues Riff"
- __ Rock and blues songs like "One-Finger Blues"
- __ Spanish-style music like "Romanza"
- __ Playing in ensembles
- __ Playing solo guitar music

49

Appendix 1
Parts of the Guitar DVD 43

Acoustic Guitar
Electric Guitar

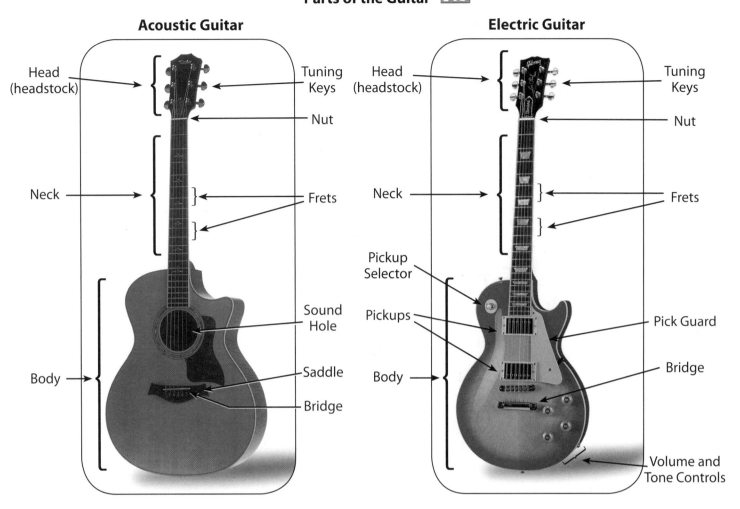

Headstocks

Guitar headstocks generally fall into two categories:

Three on a Side

Six in Line

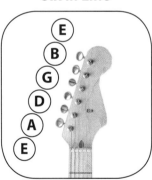

Low Strings vs. High Strings

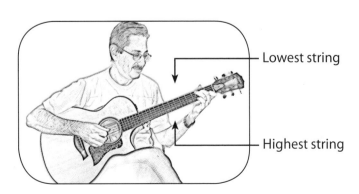

Musicians always reference "low" and "high" in relation to pitch, not the distance from the floor. So on guitar, the "lowest" sting is the thick E string which is furthest from the floor and the "highest "string is the thin E string which is closest to the floor. For the same reason, moving "up" the neck refers to moving from low notes to higher notes and moving "down" the neck refers to moving from high notes to lower notes.

Appendix 2
Guitar types

Nylon-String Acoustic

The nylon-string acoustic guitar has a softer, mellower sound than the steel-string. Nylon-string guitars are often played fingerstyle and are closely associated with Spanish, classical, and Latin American styles of guitar music.

Electric Guitar

The electric guitar is also versatile but is most often associated with rock, blues, country, and jazz music. The electric guitar works extremely well in a band situation and is usually played with a pick.

Steel-String Acoustic

The steel-string acoustic guitar is probably the most common guitar type and one of the most versatile. It is a perfect accompaniment instrument and works well played with a pick or with the fingers. It is also very appropriate for solo guitar music. The steel-string acoustic guitar can be used to perform virtually any style of music.

Appendix 3
Holding the Guitar

Sitting Position (with strap)

Sitting Position (no strap)

Right Arm

Rest your right elbow on top of the guitar as shown in the photos. Do not hang your arm in front of the guitar where it would interfere with the vibration of the guitar's top.

Classical Position

Standing Position

Appendix 4
Technique and Warm-ups

The Pick

Guitar picks are made of plastic and come in a variety of shapes, sizes, and thickness: thin, medium, and heavy. The traditional tear-drop shaped guitar pick in a medium thickness is a good choice for a beginning guitarist. Heavy picks are often preferred by electric lead guitarists, and light picks can sound especially appealing when used to strum an acoustic guitar. When using the pick, there are two distinct directions: down (toward the floor) and up (toward the ceiling). It's best to realize that the up movement is really just the result of returning your hand to its starting position—so when done properly, a down-up strum is one continuous, fluid movement, not two separate ones.

The downstrokes and upstrokes of the pick are represented with the following symbols.

Downstroke: ⊓   Upstroke: ∨

The pick should be held between the thumb and the index finger. Don't grip it tightly. The pick should be held just firm enough so that you don't drop it but lightly enough so that someone could easily remove it from your grasp. The elbow of your picking arm acts as a pivot to help you move the pick from string to string.

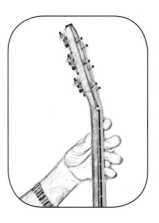

The thumb should be placed behind the neck, approximately behind your 2nd finger. The fingers should be placed directly behind the frets, not on top of them or centered between them.

Strumming and Picking Exercises

- Exercise 1: Beginning with the 6th string (the thickest one), pick each string. Use the weight of your hand and forearm to drop your pick through the string (try not to push it through) and allow it to come to rest on the next string. Then play the next string, and so on.
- Exercise 2: Now strum all six strings. Hold your pick loosely and let your hand glide rapidly through all six strings. Strive for one sound, not six separate attacks.
- Exercise 3: Try using alternating downstrokes and upstrokes to play the 1st string. Hold the pick loosely so that there is no resistance to the pick in either direction.

Fingerpicking

A pick is great for strumming and playing single-note lines, but by using your right-hand thumb and fingers together, you can create beautiful fingerpicking patterns as you hold simple chords with your left hand. Follow the technique instructions below.

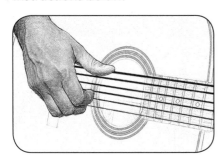

Place your left hand in playing position, but don't fret any notes. Place the right hand as follows:
- Thumb (*p*) on the 6th string
- Index finger (*i*) on the 3rd string
- Middle finger (*m*) on the 2nd string
- Ring finger (*a*) on the 1st string

Fingerpicking Technique

- The thumb should sweep through the string, towards the fingers. It should touch and bounce off the tip of the index finger. Your thumb should always be in front of your fingers, not behind them.
- Each finger should push through the string.
- Each finger should remain curved and travel in an arc from the string towards the center of your palm.
- Thumb and fingers should remain relaxed and gently curved at all times. All motion should initiate from the first knuckle joint at your palm, not from bending the middle knuckle joint at the center of your finger.

Left Arm: The Neck Wrap

A good way to establish the correct left hand position is to wrap your left hand completely around the top of the guitar neck, as in the photo on the right. This natural grasp aligns the knuckles with the strings, which is necessary for good guitar technique. Now roll your left hand toward the floor, sliding your arched fingertips down to the 1st string (nearest the floor), with your thumb remaining centered behind the neck. By keeping your knuckles aligned with the strings, especially while playing chords, you will get the best sound with the least amount of effort.

The Importance of Warming Up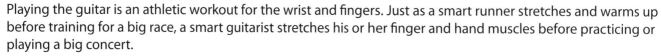

Playing the guitar is an athletic workout for the wrist and fingers. Just as a smart runner stretches and warms up before training for a big race, a smart guitarist stretches his or her finger and hand muscles before practicing or playing a big concert.

1. Gentle Finger Pull-Back and Tug

Gently pull back and stretch your hands.

Gently tug and stretch your hands.

2. Wrist Rotation

Touch the tip of your thumb to the tip of your index finger, and extend the other three fingers with the left and right hands. While keeping your elbows at your sides, rotate your hands in opposite directions several times like airplane propellers.

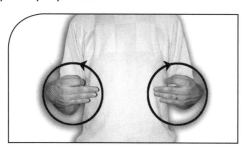 

3. 1, 2, 3 Between-the-Finger Stretch

Place your right-hand index finger between the index and middle finger of your left hand and gently massage the base of the fingers. Then add your right-hand middle finger and repeat, and finally the ring finger. Move to the next pair of left-hand fingers.

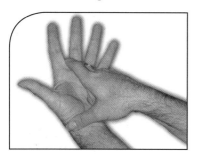  

To play chords cleanly, it is important that the nails of the left hand are kept short to allow the tips of the fingers to depress the strings. A proper length will allow your fingertips and nails to make contact with a flat surface, such as a table, at the same time.

Appendix 5
Tuning the Guitar 🔘 DVD 45

Following are several methods for tuning your guitar. No matter what tuning method you use, here are a few basic tips:

• It is always easier to tune up to the correct pitch than to tune the string down. This is because our ears seem to hear when a note is flat (below pitch) more clearly than when a note is sharp (above the correct pitch). So begin by making sure that your guitar string sounds lower than the correct pitch. If the string sounds sharp, loosen it until you know for sure that it has gone below the tuning note, and then begin to tighten it slowly, bringing it up to pitch.

• When tuning a guitar in the classroom or any noisy environment, move your ear closer to the guitar to hear your instrument more clearly.

Tuning Your Guitar to the Included CD

Your teacher has a CD with a tuning track. Beginning with your 1st string (closest to the floor), turn the correct tuning key until your string comes up to match the pitch on the CD. If necessary, bring the string flat first so that you can then tune up to the correct pitch.

Electronic Tuners

Many brands of small battery-operated tuners, similar to the ones shown, are available. Simply follow the instructions supplied with your tuner.

Clip-on tuner

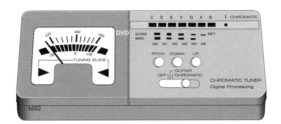

Free-standing tuner

Tuning the Guitar to a Piano

One of the easiest ways to tune a guitar is to a piano keyboard. The six strings of the guitar are tuned to the keyboard notes, as shown.

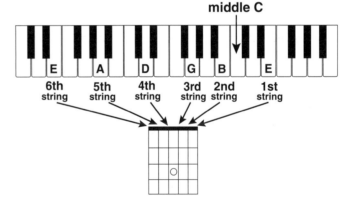

Tuning the Guitar to Itself (Relative Tuning)

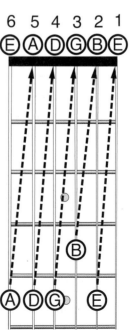

1. Tune the 6th string to E on the piano (or some other fixed-pitch instrument). You can also use a pitch pipe or an electronic guitar tuner.

2. Depress the 6th string at the 5th fret. Play it and you will hear the note A, which is the same note as the 5th string open. Turn the 5th-string tuning key until the pitch of the 5th string matches that of the 6th string.

3. Depress the 5th string at the 5th fret. Play it and you will hear the note D, which is the same note as the 4th string open. Turn the 4th-string tuning key until the pitch of the 4th string matches that of the 5th string.

4. Depress the 4th string at the 5th fret. Play it and you will hear the note G, which is the same note as the 3rd string open. Turn the 3rd-string tuning key until the pitch of the 3rd string matches that of the 4th string.

5. Depress the 3rd string at the 4th fret. Play it and you will hear the note B, which is the same note as the 2nd string open. Turn the 2nd-string tuning key until the pitch of the 2nd string matches that of the 3rd string.

6. Depress the 2nd string at the 5th fret. Play it and you will hear the note E, which is the same note as the 1st string open. Turn the 1st-string tuning key until the pitch of the 1st string matches that of the 2nd string.

Appendix 6
Reading Music and TAB Notation

There are seven natural notes. They are named for the first seven letters of the alphabet: A B C D E F G. After G, we begin again with A. Music is written on a **staff.** The staff consists of five lines with four spaces between the lines.

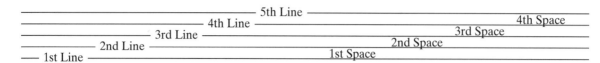

At the beginning of the staff is a **treble clef,** also called **G clef.** (The treble clef is known as the G clef because it encircles the 2nd line G.) The clef determines the location of notes on the staff. All guitar music is written on a treble clef. The notes are written on the staff in alphabetical order. The first line is E.

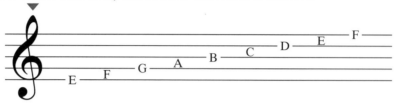

Notes can extend above and below the treble clef. When they do, **ledger lines** are added. Following is the approximate range of the guitar from the lowest note, open 6th string E, to B on the 1st string, 17th fret.

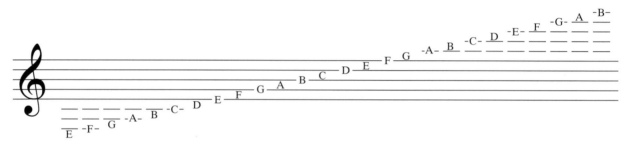

The staff is divided into measures by **bar lines.** A heavy **double bar line** marks the end of the music.

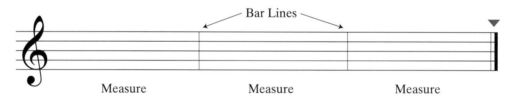

Tablature is a type of music notation that is specific to the guitar; its use dates back to the 1600s. Tablature (also known as "tab") illustrates the location of notes on the neck of the guitar. Tab is usually used in conjunction with a music staff. The notes and rhythms are indicated in the music staff; the tab shows where those notes are played on the guitar.

The location of any note is indicated by the placement of fret numbers on the strings.

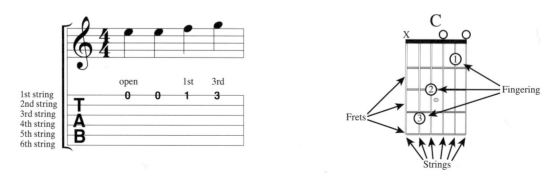

Appendix 7
Reading Rhythmic Notation

At the beginning of every song is a **time signature**. $\frac{4}{4}$ is the most common time signature:

$\frac{4}{4}$ four counts to a measure
a quarter note receives one count

Note head: **o**

Stem:

Flag:

o This is a **whole note.** The note head is open and has no stem. In $\frac{4}{4}$ time, a whole note receives four counts.

This is a **half note.** It has an open note head and a stem. A half note receives two counts.

This is a **quarter note.** It has a solid note head and a stem. A quarter note receives one count.

This is an **eighth note.** It has a solid note head and a stem with a flag attached. An eighth note receives a half count

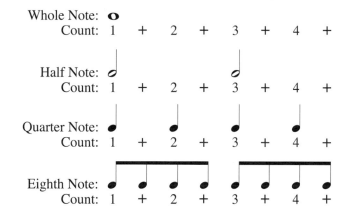

Count aloud and clap the rhythm to this excerpt from "Jingle Bells."

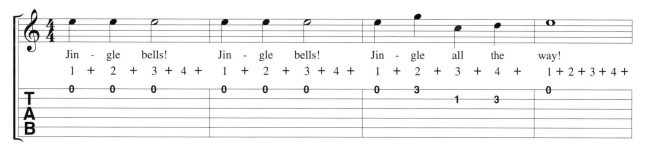

$\frac{4}{4}$ conducting pattern:

$\frac{3}{4}$ conducting pattern:

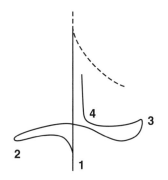

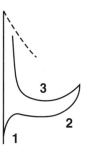

Guitar Chord Chart

A
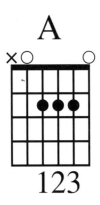
123

Am
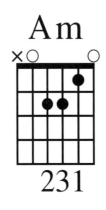
231

A7
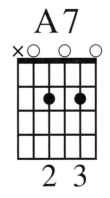
2 3

B7
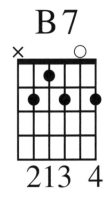
213 4

C
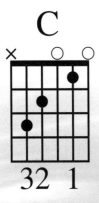
32 1

D

132

Dm
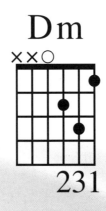
231

D7
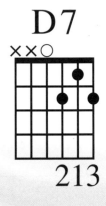
213

E
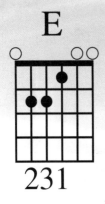
231

Em
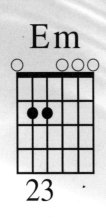
23

E7
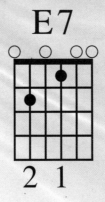
2 1

F
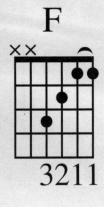
3211

G
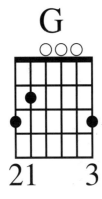
21 3

G7
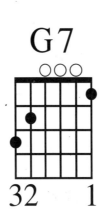
32 1

A5
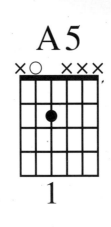
1

E5
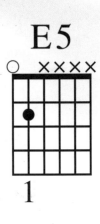
1